Elements in Intercultural Communication
edited by
Will Baker
University of Southampton
Troy McConachy
University of New South Wales, Australia
Sonia Morán Panero
University of Southampton

DIVERSITY, EQUITY, INCLUSION AND INTERCULTURAL CITIZENSHIP IN HIGHER EDUCATION

Irina Golubeva
University of Maryland Baltimore County

Shaftesbury Road, Cambridge CB2 8EA, United Kingdom

One Liberty Plaza, 20th Floor, New York, NY 10006, USA

477 Williamstown Road, Port Melbourne, VIC 3207, Australia

314–321, 3rd Floor, Plot 3, Splendor Forum, Jasola District Centre, New Delhi – 110025, India

103 Penang Road, #05–06/07, Visioncrest Commercial, Singapore 238467

Cambridge University Press is part of Cambridge University Press & Assessment, a department of the University of Cambridge.

We share the University's mission to contribute to society through the pursuit of education, learning and research at the highest international levels of excellence.

www.cambridge.org
Information on this title: www.cambridge.org/9781009565738

DOI: 10.1017/9781009442039

© Irina Golubeva 2025

This publication is in copyright. Subject to statutory exception and to the provisions of relevant collective licensing agreements, no reproduction of any part may take place without the written permission of Cambridge University Press & Assessment.

When citing this work, please include a reference to the DOI 10.1017/9781009442039

First published 2025

A catalogue record for this publication is available from the British Library

ISBN 978-1-009-56573-8 Hardback
ISBN 978-1-009-44206-0 Paperback
ISSN 2752-5589 (online)
ISSN 2752-5570 (print)

Cambridge University Press & Assessment has no responsibility for the persistence or accuracy of URLs for external or third-party internet websites referred to in this publication and does not guarantee that any content on such websites is, or will remain, accurate or appropriate.

Diversity, Equity, Inclusion and Intercultural Citizenship in Higher Education

Elements in Intercultural Communication

DOI: 10.1017/9781009442039
First published online: February 2025

Irina Golubeva
University of Maryland Baltimore County
Author for correspondence: Irina Golubeva, golubeva@umbc.edu

Abstract: Traditionally, the fields of Diversity, Equity, and Inclusion (DEI) and Intercultural Citizenship Education (ICitE) have been treated separately in Higher Education (HE) and beyond, with DEI often being associated with domestic diversity, while ICitE is often situated within international contexts. Although such binary perception is no longer adequate due to the superdiversity that characterizes today's university communities, the origins of this categorical distinction can be explained through an examination of the disciplinary roots, theoretical foundations, primary focus, and implementation approaches. Despite this difference in perspectives between the two fields, the Element argues that DEI and ICitE can complement each other in a variety of positive and productive ways. It does so by identifying the intersections between these two distinct yet interrelated fields and by providing an example of how they can be intentionally synergized in HE practice.

Keywords: intercultural citizenship education, diversity, equity, and inclusion, intercultural dialogue, empathy, higher education

© Irina Golubeva 2025

ISBNs: 9781009565738 (HB), 9781009442060 (PB), 9781009442039 (OC)
ISSNs: 2752-5589 (online), 2752-5570 (print)

Contents

1 Background   1

2 The Current Context   11

3 The Intersection of DEI and Intercultural Citizenship Education   20

4 An Example of Synergizing DEI and ICitE on a Minority-Serving Campus in the United States   46

5 Conclusions and Future Perspectives   71

References   76

1 Background

1.1 Introduction

While there are many who believe that Diversity, Equity, and Inclusion (DEI) efforts and Intercultural Citizenship Education (ICitE) can foster positive change within highly polarized societies, DEI and ICitE are not universally supported disciplines. Individuals (within and outside of Higher Education) hold skeptical views, are tired, or suffer from activist burnout (see, e.g., Chen & Gorski, 2015). Skepticism toward DEI and ICitE is unsurprising, considering our current time of uncertainty and instability where democracy has failed in many countries historically heralded as flagships of democratic practices and human rights. Beyond skepticism, the fields have also been subjected to challenges from those who reject the values the fields promote and/or are not satisfied with how these two are implemented in practice. These critiques will be expanded on in Section 2.

I begin this section by providing the Reader with a brief overview of the focus of this Element and its outline. Following that, I delve into the role of higher education (HE) and the rationale behind the importance of ICitE and DEI efforts in a globalizing world that paradoxically is experiencing increased nationalism. Additionally, I share with the Reader my positionality, which is important when discussing topics such as DEI and Intercultural Citizenship Education.

1.2 The Focus and the Outline of This Element

The objectives of this Element are threefold. First, to make a conceptual argument about how DEI and ICitE can complement each other by providing a critical overview of contemporary research and practice in the fields and investigating their intersections. Second, to demonstrate through an example of a training piloted at a US university how Intercultural Citizenship Education and Diversity, Equity, and Inclusion efforts can be synergized in the HE context. Third, to encourage Readers to become more reflective about their own institutional context and take an intentional approach to pedagogical interventions concerning DEI and ICitE.

In reference to my first objective, I maintain that a fundamental aspect of scholarly work is engagement in constructive criticism and critical (self-) reflection, where peer critique and review of scholarship allow for the exchange of diverse perspectives and offer opportunities for scholarship advancement. With regard to this, one challenge that I faced while working on this Element was trying to ensure that the critical overview – aimed at identifying opportunities for improving and synergizing the two fields –

would not be misused as an argument to undermine either of them. As previously mentioned, the fields of DEI and ICitE are currently facing critiques that are not intended to enhance their academic progress but rather to reject or discredit them. This, in particular, concerns DEI, which is the subject of significant political and ideological struggles. Given that my expertise lies in intercultural education, I am approaching my overview of both fields specifically through this lens.

Before starting the discussion on *Diversity, Equity, Inclusion and Intercultural Citizenship in Higher Education*, it is important to note that neither DEI nor ICitE can yet be classified as established academic fields in the traditional sense. However, I contend that both fit the definition of "emerging academic fields," which are typically interdisciplinary in nature and arise in response to societal, technological, or environmental changes and challenges (see, e.g., Critical Data and Algorithm Studies, Digital Humanities, Cybersecurity, Climate Policy, Cryptocurrency Studies). Despite being relatively young, DEI and ICitE have already developed a substantial body of literature that includes scholarly manuscripts, research articles, ethnographies, case studies, surveys, and textbooks. Both DEI and ICitE are present in educational curricula, offered as courses or as stand-alone academic degrees and certificate programs. Additionally, there are research centers and communities of practice conducting scholarly work and projects in DEI and ICitE, and there are professional associations that organize regular conferences, workshops, and symposia. Moreover, both DEI and ICitE have practical applications, such as in educational policymaking processes or cross-curricular collaboration. Given these accomplishments, I will refer to them as "fields" throughout this Element.

Traditionally, both within and beyond HE, these fields are treated as separate entities with ICitE being primarily associated with international diversity, and DEI with domestic. Although this binary perception is now inadequate due to the superdiversity characterizing today's higher education (and the world), the origins of their separation and distinction can be explained through exploring the disciplinary roots, theoretical foundations, primary focus, and implementation approaches for the fields. Quite often, as expanded on in this Element, intercultural education is criticized for taking an overly simplistic approach and inadequately addressing topics like power, privilege, and social justice, while DEI can be critiqued for lacking a global perspective and trying to project domestic concerns to international contexts, that is, "exporting" and "forcing" one's understanding of certain practices on another culture in ways that would not work in that culture. In the United States, for example, a common critique of how DEI concepts can be operationalized on a college campus is the introductory level of DEI "101-type" of training. These trainings tend to see everything as "black & white," "racist vs. non-racist," "inclusive vs. not inclusive." This simplistic approach can put students on the defensive (Linder, 2016) and fails to scaffold students' development (Zheng, 2022). Despite the separation between the two fields, I argue that DEI and ICitE can complement each other in a variety of positive and productive ways. In this Element, I identify relevant intersections between DEI and ICitE and shed light on how the two distinct, yet interrelated fields can be synergized in HE practice.

The Element comprises five sections, each containing a short introduction and several subsections. In Section 1, I lay the foundation of the rest of the Element by interrogating the role of HE, discussing why humanistic goals should be integrated in higher education, providing an overview of the rest of the sections, and sharing with Readers my positionality. Section 2 describes the current context of ICitE and DEI work, including policies, practices, and pitfalls. Then, Section 3 examines the two fields in more detail through explaining the theoretical foundations and briefly overviewing the history and the main concepts to ground the discussion of the intersections between ICitE and DEI. In Section 4, I share insights from the most recent research projects I led as a principal investigator that include (1) a campus-wide survey on students' experiences with diversity, equity, and inclusion as they relate to various aspects of their identity, their perceptions of the importance of intercultural and democratic citizenship competences; (2) a training initiative that can serve as an example of how DEI and ICitE can be synergized in higher education settings. In the fifth and final section, I summarize the Element, offer suggestions for future research, and share my final remarks.

I recognize that, due to the progressively increasing body of literature on DEI and ICitE, it is not possible to include an overview of all ongoing research and education projects in these two fields deserving of discussion. I trust, though, that this Element will offer sufficient insights into both, demonstrate how the efforts in the two fields can be synergized, and explain why university students and society at large would benefit from their purposeful integration into HE. The aim of this publication is thus not to persuade, nor – as the opponents of the two fields might suggest – to "indoctrinate" the audience. Instead, it aims to offer a nuanced understanding of theoretical foundations, practical applications, and potential intersections of DEI and ICitE, while acknowledging the complexities of the two fields. By sharing the insights from evidence-based analysis, this work seeks to underscore the transformative potential that emerges when these fields are intentionally integrated into HE curricula.

This Element is intended for a diverse audience, primarily composed of HE professionals, graduate students, researchers, educational consultants, trainers, international education stakeholders, and social justice advocates who are committed to fostering more inclusive, equitable, and globally minded educational environments, and who are ready to critically explore their own practices and engage in constructive critique to enhance efforts in DEI and ICitE. To support this reflective journey, I have included Thought Boxes throughout the sections, intended to foster informed dialogue and invite Readers to (self-)reflect and check their understanding and perceptions of concepts like intercultural citizenship, DEI, and social justice, among others. The goal of these Thought Boxes is not to provide definitive or "right" answers but to stimulate discussion and spur the co-construction of knowledge that respects the diversity of perspectives on the issues addressed in this Element.

1.3 The Role of Higher Education in a Globalizing World

The detailed history of universities and HE is well-documented and encompasses at least the last one thousand years. The world's oldest university (according to the Western understanding of the word), the University of Bologna in Bologna, Italy, has operated continuously since it was founded in 1088. In the United States, the oldest university, Harvard University, was founded during the period of colonization in 1636, so it is older than the founding of the United States in 1776. As societies evolved, universities likewise evolved, albeit sometimes slowly, which proves the potential of HE to embrace change and meet new challenges of the ever-developing world. Depending on historical circumstances and local conditions, universities have incrementally adapted to or have been at the forefront of societal changes. Before we continue, please take a moment to reflect on the question in Thought Box 1.

> THOUGHT BOX 1 REFLECTING ON THE PURPOSE OF HIGHER EDUCATION
>
> ▶ In your opinion, what is the purpose of HE in the twenty-first century?

A neoliberal view of HE argues that the sole purpose of universities is to prepare professionals for their careers, and that the education of future citizens falls outside their purview. Applying Hunt's (2016) definition of neoliberalism, such an instrumental approach to higher education can be described as "a project of potentiality, organizing economic and social process activity for the accumulation of capital," with explicitly stated "market-based imperatives" (2016, p. 381). The profit-driven framing of HE led to the privatization of campus facilities and services, commercialization of intellectual property, reduced staff and tenured faculty positions, and smaller salary raises, "while administrative salaries, athletic spending, and campus beautification projects have continued to escalate" (Schraedley et al., 2021, p. 3, referring to Cloud, 2018; Peck, 2015). Schraedley and colleagues (2021) refer to multiple studies (predominantly focused on US-students) that show how the neoliberal paradigm disproportionately affected the most vulnerable student populations, including ethno-racial minorities, low-income, and first-generation students, contributing to hardships, including food insecurity, health insurance issues, housing, and even homelessness (Crutchfield & Maguire, 2018; Goldrick-Rab et al., 2019; Jimenez, 2019; Pennamon, 2018, etc.).

Both philosophical and educational research literature widely critique a purely instrumental role in HE and advocate for a humanistic approach (see, e.g., Barnett, 1997, 2023; Byram et al., 2022; Lantz-Deaton & Golubeva, 2020; Nussbaum, 2002, 2006; Porto et al., 2023), opposing the opinions of those who see universities as academic silos[1] that should only equip students with knowledge and skills necessary to master the discipline of their studies.

When discussing "what is it to *be* a university?" Barnett (2011) draws on Heidegger's term "being-possible." Although there are apparently several possibilities for the university, "with possibilities comes also responsibility" (Barnett, 2011, p. 400), and the responsibility of the twenty-first century's university, according to him, is "to develop a *societal mission*, even a *global mission*" (p. 453, italics added). Barnett describes it as a university that intentionally and systematically works on "helping *to bring about a sustainable world*; and here, sustainability would be understood generously to include personal and social well-being as much as physical and material well-being" (2011, p. 454, italics added). He terms it the "ecological university" and argues that its epistemic efforts should be grounded in transdisciplinarity that includes "concern[s] for *the totality of the world*, [and] has a sense of *the interconnectedness of the world*" (Barnett, 2023, p. 126, italics added). In other words, the ecological university extends *beyond* inquiries into knowledge that is "multidisciplinary, or even interdisciplinary" (Barnett, 2023, p. 126). When scrutinizing the future of universities, Barnett proposes, therefore, a twofold thesis, which is "at once conceptual, theoretical and recommendatory," stating that:

(1) *the university should take seriously its entwinement with the world*; indeed, with large eco-systems of the world;
(2) *the instrumentality* that is so prevalent in universities *should be displaced by an ethic of collective care for the world* in which the university is entangled. (Barnett, 2023, p. 117, italics added)

---

[1] Meaning an isolated place where research and education takes place, and which has little impact on a real world.

Nussbaum (2002, 2006) also emphasizes the importance of humanistic education, drawing a clear link between humanistic education and education for democratic citizenship: "*Nothing could be more crucial to democracy than the education of its citizens*" (Nussbaum, 2006, p. 387, italics added). She argues that

> The new emphasis on "diversity" in college and university curricula is above all [...] *a way of grappling with the altered requirements of citizenship in an era of global connection*, an attempt to produce adults who can function as citizens not just of some local region or group but also, and more importantly, as citizens of a complex interlocking world – and function with a richness of human understanding and aspiration that cannot be supplied by economic connections alone. (Nussbaum, 2002, p. 292, italics added)

The concept of students as global/intercultural/world citizens[2] has gained more recognition since the beginning of the twenty-first century (see Alred et al., 2006; Baker & Fang, 2021; Barnett, 2011; Byram, 2012; Golubeva et al., 2017; Lantz-Deaton & Golubeva, 2020; Nussbaum, 2002, 2006, etc.). Therefore, students are expected "to see themselves as not simply citizens of some local region or group, but also, and above all, as human beings bound to all other human beings by ties of recognition and concern" (Nussbaum, 2006, p. 389), and "to develop a sense of responsibility or interest in the world and gain an understanding of their potential impact on the world and their relationship with it" (Barnett, 2011, p. 451). Furthermore, it is argued that such transformation of students into intercultural citizens is only possible *through civic or social action* (Byram et al., 2022). Prior research suggests that engaging in civic/social action can contribute to educating *plurilingual-and-interculturally competent democratically active citizens,* as shown through a virtual exchange project between university students in Argentina and the United States (Porto et al., 2023). Such activities do not necessarily need to happen at the international level: an intercultural citizen can take civic/social action at the local, regional, or national level (Byram & Golubeva, 2020; Golubeva, 2023).

These deliberations are not meant to disregard the value of equipping students with discipline-related knowledge and skills. If one day I needed surgery, I would hope the surgeon had learned to virtuously master a scalpel in school. What I advocate for is a *balanced and comprehensive* approach to higher education where discipline-related skills can be mastered *and* that includes a humanistic purpose, helping students mature emotionally, and preparing them for life and work in culturally diverse communities. These goals or purposes for HE do not need to be in competition with each other.

---

[2] Terms may vary and are often used interchangeably. In Section 3, I will return to the issue of terminology.

I am aware that those who believe in the purely instrumental role of HE may not see why universities should deal with DEI work and intercultural education. However, by neglecting the humanistic, they demonstrate a narrow understanding of a modern professional role, where DEI and intercultural competencies are critical job skills. As Barnett argued in his seminal book *Higher Education: A Critical Business*,

> The full-fledged professional is adept at engaging with different audiences (clients, professional peers, managers and other professionals) *through integrating critical reason, self and action*. As a professional, one has a duty to speak out to inform the public domain. Being a professional cannot be a matter solely of professional–client transactions. The professional has to engage with a wider set of discourses that generate, in turn, wider responsibilities. *In the fulfilment of those responsibilities, critical reason, critical self and critical action are united*. The extended professional is necessarily *a critical person*. (Barnett, 1997, p. 137, italics added)

In increasingly globalized societies, intercultural competence holds significant importance for employability and worker productivity (see Lantz-Deaton & Golubeva, 2020). For example, surveys showed that in Jordan, 95% of employers believed that intercultural skills are "very important"; in Indonesia and the United Kingdom, 70%; in South Africa, 63%; in India, 60%; in the United States, 58%; in the United Arab Emirates, 57%; and in Brazil, 42%; with China closing the list at 25% (British Council, 2013, p. 9). This is not surprising considering the increasing diversity in workplaces. Nowadays, it is common for job advertisements to explicitly prefer employees to have intercultural communication competence and to be committed to the values of diversity, equity, and inclusion (either explicitly or implicitly) regardless of the industry. This requirement accurately demonstrates a broader trend in the labor market of recognizing and valuing cultural diversity. For instance, in the Department of Modern Languages, Linguistics and Intercultural Communication, where I am tenured, English is not the first language for 75% of faculty members (including myself). We not only speak different World Englishes,[3] with a variety of accents, we bring a wealth of diverse perspectives and practices into our classrooms that enrich our students' understanding of the world. We navigate intercultural communication every day through varied idioms and phrasal verbs, communicative styles, and nonverbal cues. While this inevitably brings challenges in workplace communication, the advantages of our diverse workplace, including collective problem-solving and creativity, are significant.

---

[3] For definition and discussion of "World Englishes" please refer to Kachru (1997) and Jenkins (2006).

Additionally, a large study that synthesized data from over one thousand companies across twelve countries (Hunt et al., 2018) suggests that diversity enhances productivity and improves financial performance. The findings demonstrate a statistically significant correlation, revealing that companies with diverse leadership in terms of gender and ethnic/cultural representation are 21% and 33% (respectively) more likely to produce higher profits. Hence, even those who desire to pursue a purely instrumental agenda for HE cannot disregard the importance of diversity and intercultural education in the workplace. Furthermore, sustainability is a top priority for most businesses and industries, which can be achieved through integrating economic, environmental, and social perspectives into education (Jiménez-Castillo et al., 2021). Universities play an important role in Education for Sustainable Development[4] (UNESCO, 2012) and have a responsibility to prepare the next-generation workforce for a sustainable lifestyle and work through education for equality, intercultural citizenship, and human rights.

I would like to conclude Section 1.3 by quoting Barnett (2023, p. 122), who, in a very sharp and concise manner, summarized the role of the universities:

> Not only, for instance, are there conflicting ideas of democracy, rights, well-being, citizen, truth, freedom and so forth, but it is part of the role of universities to go on adding to those debates. This welter of conflicting ideas is a domain of supercomplexity (Barnett, 2000), where *disputes can never be resolved but only deepened; and deepened in part by the university itself*. (Barnett, 2023, p. 122, italics added)

1.4 Author's Background and Positionality

To you, the Reader, I want to offer a brief insight into my background and positionality that provide the foundation for my work on this Element.

My career in academia has followed a nontraditional, yet progressive, trajectory. I began as an English and Spanish language teacher, working mainly in adult and vocational education. My early research steps were inspired by intercultural interactions with my students. By the time I entered my PhD studies, I had already accumulated substantial experience as a language and intercultural educator, and these hands-on insights deeply informed my research. For a decade afterward, I combined full-time administrative leadership roles in academic affairs, project management, international education, and study abroad programs with research, teaching, and nonprofit work. Given that

---

[4] Education for Sustainable Development "empowers learners to take informed decisions and responsible actions for environmental integrity, economic viability and a just society, for present and future generations, while respecting cultural diversity. It is about lifelong learning and is an integral part of quality education" (Sandoval-Hernández et al., 2019, p. 4).

during this period I was raising two small children, while my husband served as a military doctor on peacebuilding missions, it would be more accurate to use "juggled" instead of "combined" – I felt like I was burning the candle at both ends, but this intense phase in my career provided me with invaluable learning opportunities. For instance, varied facets of my professional identity helped me see issues like internationalization from multiple, often opposing, perspectives (see Golubeva, 2020). Despite my demanding and responsibility-laden roles, a grueling schedule, and short sleeping hours, there was one aspect of my professional life I refused to give up: teaching.

The classroom, I believe, is where my most profound learning as a person and an academic takes place. I get a lot of positive vibes and useful feedback from my students. This is, I would say, where most of my own intercultural learning happens. I recall, with a touch of self-irony, stepping into my first classroom in the United States, filled with enthusiasm, curiosity, and a fair share of second-hand stereotypes. My first group of thirty undergraduate students turned out to be the most diverse I had encountered up to that point – a truly enriching experience that helped me realize how widely misguided and ideological in nature the category of a "typical American" student is.

My professional and personal experiences have inspired, enriched, and continue to inform my research, teaching, and service to the profession and the broader community. These past experiences serve as a constant reminder that the pursuit of intercultural competence is a lifelong journey. Despite having visited almost fifty countries, fluently speaking four languages, fully understanding two more, studying and working in four different countries, raising bilingual children, and living in a multicultural and plurilingual family where intercultural communication – with its whole spectrum of challenges – is a daily practice, I do not yet consider myself fully interculturally competent, nor do I believe I ever will be. Intercultural competence is inherently context-dependent, meaning in certain contexts you may be more interculturally competent, but less so in others. Furthermore, the development of intercultural competence occurs along a continuum, as described by scholars such as Bennett (1993), who outlines this process through a set of stages. It is a matter of becoming interculturally competent through experience, (self-)awareness, analysis and critical reflection. Most importantly, it is no matter how competent you become – there will always be room for further growth and improvement.

I acknowledge that this manuscript is influenced by my experiences, knowledge, and worldviews, both consciously and subconsciously. Furthermore, I anticipate that at some point, due to new experiences, knowledge, and ideological influences, some of my statements may evolve (perhaps even taking a different stance). As a scholar, I am open to this because I believe it is important to practice dialectical thought in order to recognize the value of contradiction and the limits of contemporary epistemological trends (Veraksa et al., 2022).

I consider myself an interculturalist whose research, teaching, and service to the broader community are pursuing the same overarching purpose of enhancing intercultural understanding, diversity, equity, and inclusion on campus and beyond. I was born behind the Iron Curtain and raised in an undemocratic state, so I deeply appreciate the principles of democracy. As a granddaughter of those who fought against Nazism and nationalism, I cherish their memory and appreciate their sacrifice, and I advocate for peace and civilized dialogue. Therefore, throughout my academic career, I have followed the values that reside in cultural humility, inclusiveness, and collaboration, and I have made it my mission to develop students' and my own intercultural citizenship competencies, promote peaceful solutions to conflicts, and encourage intercultural dialogue.

Being socialized in the atmosphere of constant censorship, I am particularly sensitive when I perceive freedom of speech being restricted, especially when this is done under the flag of "political correctness" and "democracy." At the same time, I do recognize that there is a risk of unrestricted freedom of speech because of hate speech that may occur. The vulnerable should be protected against expressions of hatred and incitement to violence against them. Therefore, I am very upset by the double standards adopted by the mainstream media: while, on the one hand, they advocate against hate speech, on the other hand, they demonize their opponents (this critique refers to both wings: the Left and the Right). Instead of promoting intercultural dialogue, they contribute to further dividing already strongly polarized nations, thus threatening social peace. While the degree of polarization varies between the two wings (see, e.g., Desilver, 2022; Hmielowski et al., 2020), I am concerned about people's willingness to believe whatever is said against their opponents and the lack of intercultural dialogue between opposing sides. I am also deeply troubled by the amount of fake news, misinformation, and populism (for some examples see McKenzie, 2019) that continue to mislead people (sometimes the populations of whole countries). The ability to evaluate information objectively is clouded by strong emotions. Critical thinking is shut down. Populism is on the rise.

When I advocate for freedom of speech, I advocate for freedom of thought. As Benjamin Franklin wrote 300 years ago, "Without Freedom of Thought, there can be no such Thing as Wisdom; and no such Thing as publick Liberty without Freedom of Speech" (Labaree, 1959, original spelling). Therefore, the purpose of this Element is not to impose my thinking about DEI and ICitE on the Reader, but rather to invite you to explore your own thoughts on the subject matter. I encourage you to consider multiple perspectives that could be more appropriate in your local context. Our viewpoints are shaped by our backgrounds, the privileges we have experienced, and the oppression and discrimination we have encountered. I value the opportunity to share my thoughts on DEI and ICitE in higher education, and I approach this opportunity with care, mindful that any criticism I present on the fields may be extracted from its context and used by opponents of DEI and ICitE to undermine them. I believe both fields offer value, and my critiques are in an effort to strengthen, not invalidate, them. I recognize that my understanding of these two fields is heavily influenced and limited by my (mostly) privileged personal and professional experiences. Therefore, I invite Readers to engage in an open dialogue, and I welcome constructive criticism, especially if it leads to actionable outcomes. Moreover, I am open to future collaborations.

2 The Current Context

2.1 Introduction

This section offers a brief overview of the current context of DEI and ICitE. After sharing insights on policies, practices, and pitfalls of the fields, I make a call for an intentional approach in synergizing ICitE and DEI efforts on university campuses, and I argue that the "intercultural" in Intercultural Citizenship Education needs to be dissociated from "international," and that "diversity" in DEI needs to be dissociated from "domestic."

2.2 Overview of Current Policies, Practices, and Pitfalls in DEI and ICitE

I initiate the discussion on current policies, practices, and pitfalls in ICitE and DEI work as an explicit supporter of both fields and, as mentioned in Section 1.2, I want to see them develop. I like to think that most of the Readers of this Element share the idea that there is room for improvement in both fields and believe that DEI efforts and ICitE can bring about a positive change in societies that are highly polarized, misinformed, and full of prejudices. Let us first have a closer look into the praxis[5] of Intercultural Citizenship Education and then follow with the discussion of DEI. Before reading on, please take some time to explore the mission statement, policies, and strategic plan documents at your organization or institution by reflecting on questions in Thought Box 2.

---

[5] Understood here as established practice.

> **THOUGHT BOX 2 REFLECTING ON THE MISSION STATEMENT, POLICIES, AND STRATEGIC PLAN DOCUMENTS AT YOUR ORGANIZATION OR INSTITUTION**
>
> After having explored the mission statement, policies, and strategic plan documents at your organization or institution, please reflect on the following questions:
>
> ▶ How is intercultural, global, or world citizenship articulated in these documents, if at all? How is this implemented in practice at your organization/institution? What is your level of satisfaction in this regard?
> ▶ How are diversity, equity, and inclusion articulated in these documents, if at all? How is this implemented in practice at your organization/institution? What is your level of satisfaction in this regard?
> ▶ What could be improved at your organization/institution in relation to ICitE and DEI efforts, if anything?

Important to note that how you as the Reader see both DEI and ICitE practiced is dependent on your individual (as well as institutional, and maybe political) context. For some Readers, DEI or ICitE may be associated with specific offices or positions that explicitly incorporate these fields as part of their role. While other Readers may view DEI and ICitE as a responsibility for everyone. In this Element, I have intentionally refrained from imposing what constitutes DEI and ICitE practices in higher education, as all institutions may have different needs and contexts. Instead, I encourage Readers from diverse perspectives on DEI and ICitE to engage in an open discussion and identify what is relevant and applicable to their own contexts.

2.2.1 Praxis of Intercultural Citizenship Education

It is quite common nowadays for the pursuit of global, intercultural, or world citizenship (terminology varies) to be included as a goal of HE in policy documents at institutional, national, and supranational levels. In terms of ICitE, I reflect only on the institutional level because this falls within the scope of this Element. At the institutional level, the education of global, intercultural, or world citizens is often included in university mission statements and internationalization strategy plans (Aykol et al., 2021; Lundgren et al., 2020; Woodin et al., 2011, etc.). However, these documents seldom delve into ICitE in depth. Despite a large body of research on global, intercultural, world citizenship education – institution documents tend to lack a clear definition or theoretical grounding for the terms they use. Even when the language used in the institutional policy documents can be traced back to some widely known publications – including *White Paper on Intercultural Dialogue* (CoE, 2008), *Reference Framework of Competences for Democratic Culture* (CoE, 2018), and *PISA Global Competence Framework* (OECD, 2018), – they do so in a superficial manner, remaining ambiguous in terms of implementation and evaluation. Such superficiality can give an unfortunate impression that the incorporation of citizenship education in mission statements and internationalization plans is more of a "buzz" word than an ongoing and operationalized value or institutional goal that is rooted in academic scholarship that has theory, pedagogy, implementation, and evaluation practices. Moreover, these documents often focus solely on the instrumental benefits of acquiring intercultural competence, such as better employability, neglecting the humanistic value of intercultural citizenship education.

Such articulation of intercultural (global/world) citizenship in institutional policy documents often leads to a limited, and piecemeal approach to ICitE in the everyday practices of universities, for example, by reducing it to participation in study abroad programs. Although the pursuit of intercultural citizenship is typically cited as a main goal of international mobility (Aykol et al., 2021; Baker et al., 2022; Kishino & Takahashi, 2019, etc.), the impact of studying abroad on students' civic education remains an unfulfilled promise in most of the programs (see, e.g., EC, 2019; Golubeva et al., 2018; Mitchell, 2012). This concerns even such a prominent program as ERASMUS[6] (European Region Action Scheme for the Mobility of University Students), designed to promote supranational identity and foster active citizenship (EC, 2018a). Prior research indicates that the way these programs operate does not effectively contribute to increasing students' civic responsibility (Golubeva et al., 2018). Even when study abroad experiences lead to fostering a sense of belonging to a transnational community, that sense of belonging does not necessarily translate into active civic participation. For instance, when in a study conducted among 174 ERASMUS students from 23 countries (Golubeva et al., 2018), the participants were asked about the main impact of studying abroad, "increasing civic responsibility" was the least frequently mentioned outcome (out of 16 offered response options). On both personal and professional levels, I wholeheartedly endorse the value of study abroad experiences and acknowledge that they have the potential to develop intercultural citizenship. However, the current practice of relying almost solely on study abroad programs for an institution to achieve its intercultural citizenship education goals falls short.

---

[6] The European Region Action Scheme for the Mobility of University Students (ERASMUS) was established by the European Union in 1987.

In this Element, I argue that intercultural citizenship education at universities needs to be done in a more systematic manner, and opportunities to develop one's intercultural competencies should be offered to everyone, not just those able to participate in study abroad programs. Not all students have the means to study abroad due to financial limitations, disabilities, personal circumstances, or full-time employment commitments. They should not be excluded from intercultural learning. I believe that the strong emphasis institutional internationalization strategies place on the benefits of study abroad, featuring it as "the one and only way" to develop intercultural and global competences, contributes to many students from marginalized groups feeling like outsiders. This perception leads them to believe that intercultural (global or world) citizenship is elitist beyond their reach.

On a positive note, there is a notable increase in incorporating global, intercultural, or world citizenship focus and learning outcomes at curricular level across a variety of disciplines including:

- Language education and virtual exchange (e.g., Byram et al., 2017; O'Dowd, 2020; Porto et al., 2023);
- Engineering (e.g., Dan Hirleman, 2011);
- International studies (e.g., Johnson et al., 2011);
- Medicine (e.g., Blum et al., 2019);
- Social studies (e.g., Myers, 2006; Ortloff, 2011);
- and many other areas (for further discussion see Aktas et al., 2017).

However, as Baker and Fang (2021, p. 1) rightfully point out, "the extent to which intercultural citizenship goes beyond promotion and marketing and is meaningfully incorporated into university curricula and teaching practices is still unclear. Most significantly, there is little evidence that students themselves are aware of, motivated by, or develop a sense of intercultural citizenship."

In addition to the issues discussed earlier, it is noteworthy to reflect on another key critique of ICitE. Some view Intercultural Citizenship Education as being "too" ideological or political. I believe education in general, and education for intercultural citizenship in particular, are inevitably political and ideological. Even very liberal education is still strongly ideological and politicized. Why? Because it endorses certain values (even if these values are about tolerance and appreciation of differences). In Byram, Golubeva, and Porto (2022), for instance, we suggest as a way to ensure the minimization of nationalist perspectives in language education that it should embrace internationalism (which is an ideology, too), criticality and intercultural citizenship, competencies for intercultural and democratic culture (again, ideological) (see Section 3.2 for detailed discussion). To believe otherwise would be naive.

2.2.2 Praxis of Diversity, Equity, and Inclusion

Now, let us have a look at the praxis of DEI. In the US context, commitment to Diversity, Equity, and Inclusion is often much better articulated in institutional policies than education for intercultural (global/world) citizenship. DEI efforts are often supported through law,[7] funding, and apparatus (except for the states where anti-DEI bills have been recently introduced; see Adams & Chiwaya, 2024). However, this support is experiencing pushback in the current political climate. It is noteworthy to mention that in such countries as the United States, federal and state laws can differ dramatically on this, and create a conflict that is irresolvable at the institutional level. For example,

> Florida Gov. Ron DeSantis (R) said Thursday his state "will not comply" with recently unveiled changes to Title IX by the Biden administration. "Florida rejects [President Biden's] attempt to rewrite Title IX," DeSantis said in a video posted to the social platform X. "We will not comply, and we will fight back." (Suter, 2024, web)

It is hard to predict the future, but with the rise of conservative sentiment, the number of states in the United States introducing bills to either regulate or restrict DEI initiatives is growing (see for details Adams & Chiwaya, 2024). If enacted, these bills will ban public institutions, which receive state and federal funding, from using these funds on DEI initiatives and staff. One of the main arguments underlying this legal battle is that the legislators in those states "don't want public money going to political activism" (Adams & Chiwaya, 2024). Those in favor of these restrictions argue that DEI imposes "orthodoxy" on students, "not even necessarily in the classroom, but through the administrative apparatus of the university itself"; and those against these anti-DEI bills say they "suppress[...] academic freedom and insert[...] conservative political orthodoxy into the classroom" (CBS/News Service of Florida, 2023). To grasp the nature of the current debates around DEI in academia see, for example, recently published papers by Baker (2024) and Herbert (2023), who share different opinions on DEI. Baker (2024) advocates for the principles of

---

[7] For example, in the United States *Title VII of the Civil Rights Act of 1964* (prohibiting discrimination in the workplace, including discrimination based on race, color, religion, sex (including pregnancy), national origin, age (40 or older), disability, or genetic information); *Title IX of the Education Amendments of 1972* (prohibiting sex-based employment discrimination in federally assisted schools, educational programs, and activities, see *Title VII of the Civil Rights Act of 1964 (Pub. L. 88–352)*, the *Clery Act* (requiring colleges and universities across the United States to disclose information about crime on and around their campuses, see *Jeanne Clery Disclosure of Campus Security Policy and Campus Crime Statistics Act of 1990, 20 U.S.C. §1092(f)* (2018)), etc.

individual merit and fairness. He explores a case study where a "concerned" member of a Faculty Senate at a US university requested "precise and agreed-upon" DEI definitions and "terms of reference" before voting a proposal to include DEI mandates in the Faculty Handbook, explaining this by the need "to ensure that [they] are focused on constitutional and legal agreement in what [they] are trying to accomplish" (2024, p. 2). When doing so, the Faculty Senator emphasized "the importance of clarity and legal considerations in the implementation of DEI policies compliant with the SCOTUS ruling" (Baker, 2024, p. 5), but was "verbally attacked" by the Vice President for Diversity in front of colleagues (see Baker, 2024, for full transcript). The author of the other paper (Herbert, 2023) advocates for diversity and analyzes how terms related to DEI – such as "critical race theory," "woke ideology," and "cancel culture" – are "being manipulated for political ends" (2023, p. 261). Citing more than 700 sources, Herbert (2023) challenges, among others, topics of "equity versus free speech," "academic freedom," and "the meritocracy myth." The two papers serve as an accurate reflection of the debates in Western higher education. Regardless of the side a university administration is leaning toward, one thing is certain: there is little dialogue on campuses intentionally organized to address opposing views from multiple perspectives. In practice, universities encounter many difficulties (for example, when a student organization invites on campus a speaker who is seen as a radical left or radical right) and the administration can find it challenging to foster an environment where intentional dialogue around opposing views is encouraged, so all individual students feel like they belong. This prompts the question: after funding cuts, will institutions remain committed to diversity, equity, and inclusion, or will they follow the example of the corporate world?

Just a year after George Floyd's murder (between summer 2020 and summer 2021), hiring for DEI positions spiked 92% across the United States (Hsu, 2023). In the summer of 2023, the US Supreme Court ended race-conscious college and university admissions (see for details a 237-page document on the website of the Supreme Court of the United States, 2023). This was preceded by two lawsuits that Students for Fair Admissions (SFFA) filed against Harvard College and the University of North Carolina (UNC) "to defend human and civil rights" of students of all races (SCOTUS, 2023, p. 2). SFFA argued that the race-based admissions programs of the two universities involved stereotyping of applicants based on their race and resulted in fewer admissions of Asian-American students (SCOTUS, 2023, p. 7), thus violating Title VI of the Civil Rights Act of 1964, 78 Stat. 252, 42 U. S. C. §2000d[8] *et seq.*, and the Equal Protection Clause of the Fourteenth

---

[8] Title VI provides that "[n]o person in the United States shall, on the ground of race, color, or national origin, be excluded from participation in, be denied the benefits of, or be subjected to

Amendment (SCOTUS, 2023, p. 6). Harvard College and the University of North Carolina's practices were criticized for "using racial categories that are plainly overbroad (expressing, for example, no concern whether South Asian or East Asian students are adequately represented as "Asian"); arbitrary or undefined (the use of the category "Hispanic"); or underinclusive (no category at all for Middle Eastern students)" (SCOTUS, 2023, pp. 6–7). Although the US Supreme Court decision regarded affirmative action in HE settings, the companies that never believed DEI a priority used it as "a moment to get out" (Hsu, 2023). Within just a couple of months, the number of DEI job announcements dropped by 38% (Hsu, 2023). One may only speculate on how all of these will influence university DEI policies and practices, especially given that many institutions pursue a neoliberal agenda, as discussed in Section 1 of this Element.

Undoubtedly, there is a considerable degree of divisiveness surrounding the discussion on DEI. Even within organizations that generally endorse and advocate for Diversity, Equity, and Inclusion efforts, there is noticeable "DEI fatigue" (Bhasin, 2022; Laing, 2022; Rae, 2023; Willingham, 2022). For example, according to a campus climate survey at one of the universities in the United States, more than a quarter of faculty and staff (27%) believe that "DEI distracts from achieving [the university's] academic mission," and more than one-third of respondents (36%) thought that "there is too much emphasis put on issues of diversity, equity, and inclusion" (UI, 2022, p. 6). Although the overall percentage of respondents agreeing that their university is "strongly committed to DEI" is very high (83%), a discernible average decrease of 8% has been observed in the course of four years between 2018 and 2022 (UI, 2022, p. 6). Interestingly, among faculty and staff, the most significant decrease was observed among postdocs; and among students, the most critical were the graduate students (UI, 2022, p. 26).

Willingham, an expert in DEI, explains the situation by multiple causes and I am highlighting the three ones that are relevant to our discussion. First, she mentions lack of training, rightfully pointing out that "[...] DEI roles require specialized training and a high degree of expertise. You can't just expect someone to perform well in a DEI role because they are the only multicultural person on your team" (Willingham, 2022, web). Second, there is an observable disconnect between values and implementation. Discrimination and microaggressive behavior remain present despite numerous DEI training sessions, raising the question of whether DEI training is impactful for reducing discrimination and harm. For example, a compulsory "Responsible Employee" training on Policy on Sexual

---

discrimination under any program or activity receiving Federal financial assistance." 42 U. S. C. §2000d. (SCOTUS, 2023, p. 6).

Misconduct, Sexual Harassment and Gender Discrimination, which relates to three acts (Title IX, Title VII, and the Clery Act), is designed for thirty minutes only. To pass the required training and become a "responsible employee"/a "good citizen" of the campus community, one has to complete two five-question quizzes with a score of 80% or higher. The questions in these quizzes mainly focus on "responsible" reporting procedures. To me, this type of DEI work appears to be more about educating on compliance requirements than educating on "good citizenship." This is closely connected to the third problematic issue from Willingham's list, that is, that there is a greater focus on compliance and appearances rather than on sustainable transformation:

> Social justice movements have fueled a reactive urgency and pressure for DEI initiatives, forcing many diversity leaders to focus on vanity metrics and social media messaging over sustainable, long-term change. This isn't to say your company can't engage in public-facing DEI work, but keep in mind how demoralizing DEI work can feel when leaders act more like PR agents than internal changemakers. (Willingham, 2022, web)

I would like to conclude Section 2.2 by acknowledging that the discussion of policies, practices, and pitfalls in the fields of ICitE and DEI would deserve a separate study and that I recognize that the scope of this section is limited to some general insights and examples from the US context. However, my hope is that the Reader has been presented with a sufficient argument to understand my call for revising the current approaches to ICitE and DEI.

2.3 A Call for an Intentional Approach in Synergizing ICitE and DEI Efforts

After having briefly discussed the challenges that the fields of ICitE and DEI currently experience, I move now to the central argument of the Element: that the efforts of the two fields need to be synergized, meaning their combined efforts will achieve better outcomes together than if pursued separately. I see the solution in shifting to more intentional pedagogical interventions for both DEI and ICitE and integrating them into higher education curricula.

From my personal and professional experience, the current practices in HE primarily indicate an almost complete lack of communication between the fields of ICitE and DEI. (I would appreciate it if the Readers could counter this by offering examples of good practices implemented at their institutions.) This issue does not stem from a lack of ability for the two fields to communicate, or from the fields having opposing values and ideals but rather it stems from organizational choices like being placed in separate departments/offices, having distinct agendas, and applying different methods. One reason for such separation is the reliance on a traditional view that primarily associates Intercultural Citizenship Education with international diversity and DEI with domestic. As discussed in the introductory section of this Element, this binary perception is inadequate due to the superdiversity of university campuses (and most of the societies in the world). Limiting the scope of ICitE and DEI, respectively, to international and domestic student communities creates oversimplification and inherently leads to overlooking major issues.

On the part of DEI, one significant limitation – related to this binary perception – is its frequent lack of a global perspective and the perception that it essentializes individuals based on certain aspects of their identity while (potentially) disregarding other important factors. For example, in addressing issues of racial diversity and equity, a DEI initiative may primarily focus on the Black–White racial dynamic prevalent in the US context, potentially overlooking the complex and varied experiences of individuals from other racial or ethnic backgrounds, as well as global perspectives on race and ethnicity. When discussing "where 'diversity training' goes wrong," Griffin (2021) shares the following critique,

> Often, we interact with people who have done a lot of "diversity training" but have never thought about Native Americans or Indigenous populations. They've never reckoned with the fact that Indigenous people are some of the poorest communities in the country, that they are the most likely to die from Covid-19, that they are marginalized and stereotyped in school curricula, that they are killed by police at higher rates than even Black people, that the land we live on was almost certainly stolen from these communities, that most of the people we call Latino/a/x are descended from Indigenous Americans, and that Indigenous people have been leaders in the climate justice movement and have articulated how environmental injustice is inextricably linked to racism, classism, and ableism. [...] Similarly we have participants who have done tons of race trainings but do not know the difference between race and ethnicity, [and] do not understand the difference between Latina/o/x and Hispanic. (Griffin, 2021, web)

This limited scope can hinder efforts to truly understand and address the intersectional nature of identity and discrimination on a wider scale. It is also important to note that some critiques directed at DEI are not about issues with how it is implemented but rather reject the field's values, claiming that DEI attempts to "indoctrinate" students (cf. Hanley, 2023 and Rufo, 2023). As highlighted in Section 2.2.2, DEI discussions have become heavily politicized. It is unlikely that those who are opposed to the values of DEI would find synergizing DEI and ICitE a valid answer to their criticism. However, a more nuanced and globally informed approach to DEI is essential for fostering greater inclusivity and equity within diverse communities. In this regard, the non-essentialist approach advocated by

Intercultural Citizenship Education can be very useful, as well as ICitE viewing the development of competence as a continuum (see Section 1.4).

This does not mean, though, that ICitE is flawless. Frequently, Intercultural Citizenship Education faces criticism for adopting an overly simplistic approach, failing to adequately address complex topics such as power dynamics, privilege, and social justice. Andreotti (2011) raises concerns regarding "soft" educational approaches that "fail to engage in examinations of power relations" (2011, p. 219). This is what ICitE could learn from DEI.

I strongly believe that closer collaboration between these two fields would be immensely beneficial for students for a variety of reasons. Primarily, it would:

- help them cope with value-level conflicts,
- teach them to collaborate effectively across differences,
- support them in becoming more open to diverse worldviews.

Intercultural Citizenship Education would develop empathy and perspective-taking, as well as understanding of and engaging with issues of global concern; while DEI work would ensure that this understanding and active engagement is grounded in principles of social justice and the recognition of power imbalances. This synergy would create a more equitable and inclusive community on campus and beyond. Ultimately, it would equip students with the competencies necessary to live peacefully in multicultural communities. To convince the Reader that this is feasible, in Section 3, I provide an overview of the two fields and their intersections, and in Section 4, I share an example of how ICitE and DEI can be synergized in practice, supporting this claim with both qualitative and quantitative assessment findings.

3 The Intersection of DEI and Intercultural Citizenship Education

3.1 Introduction

In this section, I summarize how the concepts of ICitE and DEI evolved over time and provide a brief overview of the history of both fields.

Starting with ICitE, I first explain the context – that of foreign language education – in which the notion of ICitE arose and was coined (Alred et al., 2006; Byram, 2008, 2012, 2014; Byram & Golubeva, 2020; Porto, 2019; Porto et al., 2018, etc.), and informed a number of important theoretical and pedagogical developments in areas such as:

- study abroad and English language teaching (e.g., Baker et al., 2022; Baker & Fang, 2021, 2022; Boonsuk & Fang, 2023; Fang & Baker, 2018; Ra et al., 2022);

- transnational telecollaborative projects (e.g., Byram et al., 2017; Golubeva & Porto, 2022; O'Dowd, 2020; Peraza & Furumura, 2022; Porto & Yulita, 2017; Porto et al., 2023; Trapè, 2019);
- service learning in language classroom (e.g., Rauscher & Byram, 2018; Rauscher & Mustroph, 2022);
- teacher training (e.g., Dooly, 2006; Palpacuer-Lee et al., 2018; Wagner et al., 2019);
- policy frameworks (e.g., Barrett, 2016; CoE, 2018).

Section 3.2 discusses DEI and, in particular, how the concept of "diversity" has significantly expanded over time. I provide a brief overview of the history of DEI, rooted in the civil rights movement. Its trajectory will be traced from the 1960s to the 1970s, when the main focus was on antidiscrimination legislation (for example, demanding access to HE for Black Americans), to a shift toward sensitivity and awareness training in the 1980s–90s, followed by adding a new (more instrumental) aspect that views diversity as an opportunity to attract "the best and the brightest" to universities and workplaces that emerged in the 2000s. In the past decade, the focus has been mainly on compliance (for example, Title IX training at US universities). Today, it is time to start thinking in terms of sustainability (UNESCO, 2012, 2014), for instance, how we can contribute to sustaining our planet by bringing together diverse perspectives and approaches to problem-solving and by learning to collaborate across differences. This is where DEI and ICitE can complement each other.

In the final section (3.4), I discuss the points of intersection, along which DEI and ICitE can be synergized, and why this would be mutually beneficial.

3.2 The Key Concepts of ICitE and the Brief History of the Field

I start Section 3.2 with clarification of its key concept – *Intercultural Citizenship Education* – that I define as "education that facilitates the development of values, attitudes, skills, knowledge and critical understanding necessary for one to be able to interact with people from other (lingua)cultures[9] in a multicultural community, both locally and globally, in a democratic and interculturally competent way" (Golubeva, 2022, pp. 191–192).

The Reader may wonder, "Why 'intercultural citizenship' and not 'global'?" As explained in Golubeva (2022), in some contexts, these two terms are used interchangeably, like when taking into consideration the need to adjust to the

---

[9] The term implies close relationship between language and culture, that the two are intertwined, and that languages are intimately related to past knowledge, local and historical context, cultural information, habits, and behaviors. (See Agar (1994) on "languaculture," and Risager (2006, 2007) on "linguaculture" – these terms are used interchangeably.)

vocabulary of research participants who may not be familiar with these terminologies (see, e.g., Golubeva et al., 2017; Han et al., 2017), or when the documents are meant for the broader community (see, e.g., OECD, 2018; UNESCO, 2014). There are some other widely used terms to denote citizenship that transcends the nation-state. According to a Google search conducted on March 9, 2024 (6:30 pm EST), the most commonly used phrases include "global citizenship" (10,000,000), "world citizenship" (1,090,000), and "cosmopolitan citizenship" (347,000). The term "intercultural citizenship" (94,600) is less commonly used and can be found mainly in digital sources related to the field of Language and Intercultural Communication Education.

So why prioritize using "intercultural citizenship" over other aforementioned terms, including the most widely used one: "global citizenship"? Before moving on to the discussion of this question, please take a moment to reflect on your citizenship affiliation in Thought Box 3.

THOUGHT BOX 3 REFLECTING ON YOUR ROLE AS A CITIZEN

Please summarize, in a few words, what do(es) your citizenship(s) mean to you?

How do you see yourself as a citizen of

▶ your local community (e.g., your street, your part of town)

....
....
....

▶ your region (e.g., part of the country where you live)

....
....
....

▶ your nation(s) (that is, in relationship to your country/ies of citizenship)

....
....
....

▶ the international community

....
....
....

THOUGHT BOX 3 (cont.)

▶ your online community (e.g., professional or social networking, virtual profile, online gaming)

....
....
....

Which of the above affiliations/memberships are important for you?

Do you consider yourself a global, world, cosmopolitan, or intercultural citizen? And why?

(Adapted from *A Portfolio of Competences for Democratic Culture* (Byram et al., 2021))

There are three main considerations for prioritizing "intercultural citizenship," each offering a different rationale, as previously discussed in Golubeva (2022).

The first rationale is *theoretical*. The field of Intercultural Citizenship Education emerged from Byram's theory of language pedagogy. Specifically, Byram's conceptualization of "intercultural (communicative) competence" (Byram, 1997, 2021) and "education for intercultural citizenship" (Byram, 2008, 2012). The idea of incorporating ICitE into the foreign language curriculum brought political and ideological dimensions into the realm of Foreign Language Teaching. Most of the research on intercultural citizenship is closely related to Language and Intercultural Communication Education (see, e.g., Alred et al., 2006; Baker et al., 2022; Baker & Fang, 2021, 2022; Byram et al., 2017; Byram et al., 2022; Golubeva, 2023; Fang & Baker, 2018; Humphreys, 2023; McConachy et al., 2022; Porto, 2019; Porto et al., 2018; Porto & Yulita, 2017; and many others). Global citizenship education, as theorized in UNESCO (2014) and the *OECD PISA Global Competence Framework* (OECD, 2018), takes a different approach, by adding to intercultural and political dimensions economic, environmental, and ecologic ones (see for details *Sustainable Development Goals,* UNDP, 2018).

The second rationale is *philosophical*. It ponders the ethical dilemma discussed by Dower (2008) on whether we *all* are global citizens or if just *some* of us are global citizens. According to Dower, "in some respects we are all global citizens, for instance because of a certain moral or legal status, but in other respects only some people are global citizens by virtue of their self-descriptions and/or active engagement with the world" (2008, p. 39). In other words, "global citizenship" is not inherently connected to education. One can be a "global citizen" from merely living on Earth, or from self-identifying as someone who believes they have a responsibility for global issues and take social/civic action to help resolve those problems. On the contrary, for one to become an "intercultural citizen," education (both inside and outside of the classroom) is essential. It is needed to raise one's critical cultural (self-)awareness and to equip them with a set of values, attitudes, skills, knowledge and critical understanding.

The third rationale is *pragmatic*. It concerns the prominent use of the term "global citizenship" in institutional mission statements and strategic plans in contexts specifically related to study abroad programs as a promise and the main outcome (see, e.g., Aktas et al., 2017; De Wit, 2010; Streitwieser, & Light, 2016; Woodin et al., 2011). A close association of the term with initiatives like study abroad, where many students cannot participate, makes the term sound elitist. Additionally, in many parts of the world, "global" holds negative connotations from its association with "globalist" and "globalization." Finally, it deviates the focus away from a systematic way of incorporating intercultural citizenship in university curricula, especially in addressing domestic diversity.

Ultimately, though in practice the terms have been often applied interchangeably, they represent distinct concepts. Based on the previously discussed arguments, I consider "intercultural citizenship" to be a more suitable term for discussing the subject matter of this Element.

The concept of "intercultural citizen" evolved from the concept of "intercultural speaker." Byram (1997) initially developed a model of intercultural (communicative) competence, aiming to shift the focus of language learning from the traditional aspiration of a "native-speaker" ideal toward becoming an intercultural speaker who is able to mediate "between" linguacultures (Risager, 2007). This change in paradigm meant that instead of speaking or behaving like a native speaker, the language learner would assume a metaphorical "third place." Adapted and applied to language education by Kramsch (1993), the concept of "third place" suggested adopting a new intermediary perspective that allows deeper understanding between one's own and the other speaker's linguaculture.[10]

Byram's model played a crucial role in shifting the instrumental understanding of intercultural (communicative) competence from being a tool for effective and appropriate communication with people from other countries (for example, for business purposes) to a humanistic perspective, which views it as a requisite for living peacefully in a multicultural environment (see Byram, 2018). In articulating the humanistic dimension, Byram (2018) underscores the importance of not only equipping individuals with skills, attitudes, and knowledge but also with internationalist values that promote mutual understanding, cooperation, peace,

---

[10] Kramsch's later work shifted emphasis toward the analysis of power in linguistic interaction and the implications for applied linguistics and language education (see Kramsch, 2020).

prosperity, and democracy (for a detailed discussion of *internationalism,* please refer to Elvin, 1960; Goldmann, 1994; Halliday, 1988). It is important to mention that internationalism is "aspirational" (Halliday, 1988) and "may never be attained but provides education with much needed moral direction" (Byram & Golubeva, 2020, p. 82). With this humanistic perspective in mind, intercultural citizenship is a normative orientation that can be implemented following democratic principles. The progression of aligning intercultural competence with democratic principles is thoroughly outlined in Barrett and Golubeva (2022).

Byram's (1997, p. 34) model of intercultural competence described five factors: (1) attitudes of relativizing oneself and valuing others; (2) knowledge of self and others and of individual and societal interaction; (3) skills of interpreting and relating; (4) skills of discovering and/or interacting; and (5) critical cultural awareness. *Critical cultural awareness* – placed at the center of this model and explicitly associated with political education – made this model particularly relevant for intercultural citizenship education because it involves critical reflection, analytical thinking, and (self-)awareness. Byram defines it as "[a]n ability to evaluate critically and on the basis of explicit criteria, perspectives, practices and products in our own and other cultures and countries" (Byram, 1997, p. 53). It is important to note that this model was not intended to incorporate all possible factors that might be necessary in intercultural interactions. Rather, it was meant to simplify and schematize competence while providing suggestions on how to teach and assess it (Byram, 2021). To achieve this aim, Byram (1997) "translated" the five factors into concrete objectives for teaching and assessing purposes (1997, pp. 50–53). For the specific purposes of interacting using a foreign language, Byram (1997) proposed a model of intercultural communicative competence, which in addition to five factors of intercultural competence, includes linguistic, sociolinguistic and discourse competences (1997, p. 73).

Since its publication, Byram's model has served as both an inspiration and a foundational reference for developing new theoretical frameworks in numerous international initiatives focused on intercultural (citizenship) education. For example, the *Autobiography of Intercultural Encounters* (AIE) (Byram et al., 2009a) is a pedagogical tool developed to help students reflect critically on their encounters – either face-to-face or through the Internet – with people from diverse ethnic, racial, religious, linguistic, and other backgrounds. The AIE competence model (Byram et al., 2009b) encompassed all five original components of Byram's model and additional components like (1) *tolerance for ambiguity,* (2) *empathy,* (3) *action orientation,* and (4) *acknowledgment of the identities of others.* These elements had been discussed in Byram (1997) but not embedded in his model (for details, please refer to Barrett & Golubeva, 2022, pp. 67–69). According to the AIE model, *acknowledging the identities of others* involves acceptance of their values and insights, and *tolerance for ambiguity* means "accepting that, because people who belong to different cultures have different beliefs and different values, there can be multiple perspectives on and interpretations of any given situation" (Byram et al., 2009b, p. 5).

This theoretical development was succeeded by the work on the project titled *Developing Intercultural Competence through Education* (DICE) (see Barrett et al., 2014). The novelty of the DICE approach lies in its explicit adoption of a non-essentialist view, which recognizes the intersectionality of multiple cultural affiliations and identities, acknowledges the dynamic nature of these cultures and identities, and emphasizes the subjective and context-dependent salience of certain cultural practices, values, norms, and beliefs (see for discussion Barrett & Golubeva, 2022, pp. 69–73). But explicitly, values were articulated in the *Reference Framework of Competences for Democratic Culture* (RFCDC) (CoE, 2018), which combines intercultural and democratic competences.

The *Reference Framework of Competences for Democratic Culture* integrates the conceptualization of "culture" as outlined in DICE. Recognizing the complex and contested nature of the term "culture" – which has been the subject of ongoing debates in the fields of social sciences and intercultural communication education – the RFCDC summarizes the main aspects of cultures as follows (CoE, 2018, Vol. 1, p. 30):

- Cultures can be interpreted through three types of resources: (1) *material*, for example, tools, artifacts, and cuisine; (2) *social*, for example, language and behavioral norms of conduct; and (3) *subjective*, for example, beliefs systems and values.
- Cultures vary in size and distinctive features. For example, they can be large religious groups, certain types of sexual orientation groups, specific disability groups, or small neighborhood communities, and so on.
- Cultures are characterized by considerable internal diversity, with boundaries being typically quite "fuzzy" because we all hold multiple identities that intersect in a unique way.
- Cultures are dynamic given that (1) they can evolve as a result of socio-economic, political, or historical events; (2) our perceived identification with particular groups can shift based on the subjective salience of our identities, and (3) they are challenged internally by their members in terms of values, norms, and practices.

The previously discussed understanding of cultures suggests that whether we perceive a particular situation as *intra*cultural or *inter*cultural depends on if we or

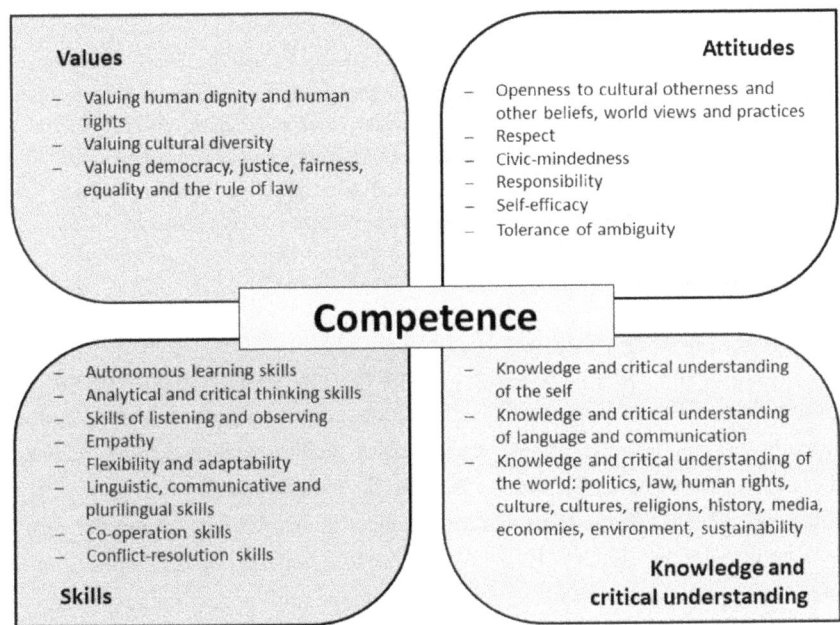

Figure 1 The 20 components of the RFCDC competence model.
Source: CoE, 2018, Vol. 1, p. 38. © Council of Europe, reproduced with permission.

others perceive ourselves as members of the in-group or out-group.[11] This perception then determines which competences will be needed in the particular situation.

The 20 RFCDC competences needed to be able to act as an active democratic and interculturally competent citizen (see Figure 1) were determined through an extensive examination of more than 100 established conceptual schemes and models of civic, democratic, and intercultural competences (for the complete list of used sources, see CoE, 2016, pp. 59–67).

The twenty areas of competence within this framework – that may be termed *intercultural and democratic competence* – are organized into four categories: (1) values, (2) attitudes, (3) skills, (4) knowledge and critical understanding. The RFCDC understands "competence" as "the ability to mobilise and deploy relevant values, attitudes, skills, knowledge and/or understanding in order to respond appropriately and effectively to the demands, challenges and opportunities that are presented by a given type of context" (CoE, 2018, Vol. 1, p. 32). The difference between "intercultural" and "democratic" is explained, as follows:

- "democratic competence" is the ability to mobilise and deploy relevant psychological resources (namely values, attitudes, skills, knowledge and/

---

[11] For discussion of in-group/out-group, please refer to Tajfel & Turner (1979).

or understanding) in order to respond appropriately and effectively to the demands, challenges and opportunities presented by democratic situations.

– Likewise, "intercultural competence" is the ability to mobilise and deploy relevant psychological resources in order to respond appropriately and effectively to the demands, challenges and opportunities presented by intercultural situations. In the case of citizens who live within culturally diverse democratic societies, intercultural competence is construed by the Framework as being an integral component of democratic competence. (CoE, 2018, Vol. 1, p. 32)

In real-life situations, the 20 RFCDC areas of competence are usually mobilized and deployed not all at once, but in clusters. The clusters represent varying combinations of values, attitudes, skills, knowledge and critical understanding, depending on the specific context. Examples of scenarios when different clusters of competences were applied can be found in the RFCDC publication (CoE, 2018, Vol. 1, pp. 32–35). To demonstrate, let us reflect on happenings during the global crisis brought on by the COVID-19 pandemic. It unveiled people's dispositions in relation to their values, attitudes, skills, knowledge and critical understanding as citizens. Do you remember politicians partying with their friends while forcing strict lockdowns on the rest of the population (Kennedy, 2022), anti-lockdown protests around the world (Carothers, 2020), harsh scenes of desperate people in China, rioting for food (ABC News Australia, 2022; Guardian News, 2022)? If not, take a moment to check these sources and answer the questions in Thought Box 4.

Another key concept that Intercultural Citizenship Education builds upon is *intercultural dialogue*. It "enables us to move forward together, to deal with our

---

THOUGHT BOX 4 REFLECTING ON CITIZENSHIP IN TIMES OF CRISIS: BEHAVIOR DURING THE COVID-19 LOCKDOWN

First, please check these news reports (ABC News Australia, 2022; Carothers, 2020; Guardian News, 2022; Kennedy, 2022).

▶ Based on the information shared in these sources, how would you describe their behavior as citizens?
▶ What 20 RFCDC competences (Figure 1) did they demonstrate (or fail to demonstrate)?
▶ How would an intercultural citizen behave in the described situations?
▶ How would you behave, or how did you behave in these situations?
▶ What did you learn about yourself and your close community during the COVID-19 lockdown?

different identities constructively and democratically on the basis of shared universal values" (CoE, 2008, p. 2). Intercultural dialogue presupposes that people have shared values that allow them to mediate between different cultures (and linguacultures) and diverse (sometimes conflicting) perspectives (Byram & Golubeva, 2020). It is recognized as a tool that "allow[s] us to prevent ethnic, religious, linguistic and cultural divides" (CoE, 2008, p. 15) and "may significantly contribute to the improvement of democracy and the development of greater and deeper inclusivity and sense of belonging" (EP, 2015, web).

The three volumes of RFCDC (CoE, 2018) provide a comprehensive overview of the model. They explain the conceptual reference framework of the competences one needs to become and act as an active intercultural citizen, provide scaled descriptors for all of the twenty components of the RFCDC model, and suggest how the model and the descriptors can be incorporated and implemented in the curriculum, pedagogy, assessment, using of a "whole school" approach. This model is relevant to working on various topics, including diversity, equity, inclusion, and social justice. For example, a pilot study involving pupils from Bulgaria, Italy, Norway, Romania, and Spain (Tenenbaum et al., 2023) examined whether a novel curriculum based on RFCDC could increase children's endorsement of children's rights. Although the RFCDC derives from a European tradition, it has been successfully applied outside the European and Western context in diverse educational settings to foster intercultural dialogue and to teach individuals to act as responsible democratic citizens. For examples of successful application of the RFCDC in intercultural citizenship education in diverse contexts, please see projects completed in Argentina and the United States (Golubeva, 2023; Golubeva & Porto, 2022), and the Global Peace Path project that involved participants with refugee status from Afghanistan, Mali, Nigeria, Senegal, Sierra Leone, Somalia, Pakistan, and Syria, cooperating with international students from Bulgaria, China, Chile, Hong Kong, Japan, Russia, Serbia and the United States (Rauschert & Mustroph, 2022).

Among the myriad concepts integral to Intercultural Citizenship Education, I would like to clarify two additional ones: "empathy" and "perspective-taking," which bear close relevance to the research findings discussed in Section 4, and are also critical to Diversity, Equity, and Inclusion. Empathy and perspective-taking play an essential role in one's ability to communicate successfully with people from diverse backgrounds (Guntersdorfer & Golubeva, 2018). They aid students in suspending judgment to understand someone else's cultural perspective:

> While you must accept that you will never truly know what others experience, you can try to put yourself in another person's shoes and imagine what it would be like to be them in order to begin to see the world from their perspective, rather than yours, and begin to empathize with their situation.
> (Lantz-Deaton & Golubeva, 2020, p.145)

Listed in most models of intercultural competence (e.g., Deardorff, 2006; Fantini, 2009; Gudykunst, 1993; Ting-Toomey & Kurogi, 1998), as well as in AIE (Byram et al., 2009b), DICE (Barrett et al., 2014), and RFCDC (CoE, 2018), empathy can be viewed as both a prerequisite for understanding people from other backgrounds and an outcome of contact with outgroup members (see Stephan et al., 1999). In the context of intercultural communication, *empathy* can be defined as "'the ability to regulate emotions, cope, and react appropriately in an intercultural encounter' by understanding and interpreting the feelings of the communication partner, who has a different cultural background and mindset" (Golubeva & Guntersdorfer, 2020, p. 119, referring to Guntersdorfer & Golubeva, 2018, p. 57).

Perspective taking – a cognitive construct of empathy – is "the tendency to spontaneously adopt the psychological view of others in everyday life" (Davis, 1983, pp. 113–114). I consider this ability to take the perspective of others particularly important for building sustainable societies and fostering intercultural dialogue in times of increased polarization (Golubeva, 2023). While it may be challenging and even uncomfortable to take the perspective of others, it is essential for conflict resolution and problem-solving. A recent study conducted among undergraduate students who engaged in intercultural citizenship telecollaboration in the United States (Golubeva, 2023) demonstrated a significant increase in both empathy and perspective-taking. Another study (Golubeva, in press) showed that increased empathy and improved perspective-taking skills contributed to enhancing students' sense of belonging and their perception of campus inclusiveness (please refer to Section 4 for further discussion).

In this section (3.2), we have briefly overviewed the history of how the field of ICitE evolved from Foreign Language Education and clarified the key concepts of intercultural citizenship education, culture, critical cultural awareness, competence, intercultural and democratic competence, intercultural vs global citizenship, intercultural dialogue, tolerance for ambiguity, empathy, and perspective-taking ability. In concluding this section, I would like to reiterate a principle from my positionality statement: the journey toward becoming an intercultural citizen is a continual commitment and moral dedication. Following Barnett's definition (1997, see discussion earlier), a *critical person* will never deem themselves a fully competent intercultural citizen. The ever-changing world brings new challenges, requiring socially responsible behavior and prompting a continuous inner dialogue concerning ethical considerations.

3.3 The Key Concepts of DEI and the Brief History of the Field

Section 3.3 takes a closer look at the field of DEI. The concepts of diversity, equity, and inclusion are widely discussed within HE and in society at large through the media, politics, organizations, and various industries (e.g., healthcare). In this section, I examine the key concepts of DEI and provide a brief overview of its history, predominantly focusing on examples from the US context, where I am geographically based. Therefore, before you continue reading, I invite you to take a moment to reflect on your local context in Thought Box 5.

> THOUGHT BOX 5 REFLECTING ON YOUR UNDERSTANDING AND PERCEPTION OF DIVERSITY, EQUITY, INCLUSION, AND SOCIAL JUSTICE
>
> ▶ How often do you hear such concepts as "DEI," "diversity," "equity," "inclusion," and "social justice"?
> ▶ How often do you use them, and for what purpose (for example, to comply with your institution's policies or to advocate for yourself or someone else)?
> ▶ What do these terms mean to you specifically? (Please critically reflect on how your understanding and perception of DEI may be influenced by the privileges or oppression you have experienced.)
> ▶ What personal or professional experiences have you had related to the discussions on DEI issues?
>
> Please define each of these terms in your own words before you continue reading this Element.

It is noteworthy that the degree to which HE institutions and states as a whole pay attention to DEI varies across the globe and even within the same county or geographic region. In some countries, like the United States, DEI efforts can be supported (or rejected) through law, and HE institutions may have funding to hire staff focused on DEI work or be barred from hiring DEI-focused positions. In other countries, these concepts may be unfamiliar and associated with the Western world. Additionally, the concept of DEI can be expanded to DEIA, which stands for Diversity, Equity, Inclusion, and Accessibility, or DEIB, which stands for Diversity, Equity, Inclusion, and Belonging, among numerous others. Again, this depends on the focus of a given institution/state, as well as the specific context and dimensions of local diversity (ethno-racial or gender equity, migrant and refugee crisis, etc.). While acknowledging the importance of the nuanced approach, in this publication, the most general acronym "DEI" is used throughout.

The acronym "DEI" has become ubiquitous but with varying meanings and values. The way it is used in different political discourses often reveals the ideological views and positionality of the speaker. Ideally, one would assume that the words "diversity," "equity," and "inclusion" would not carry any negative connotations; however, there is currently a heated anti-DEI narrative in politics and ideologies in many countries across the globe. For example, in a recent scandal involving the resignation of the president of Harvard University (Glanzman, 2024; Schuessler et al., 2024), DEI-based hiring was "blamed" for her hiring in the first place (Abcarian, 2024).

Let us review what DEI actually means through a discussion of the key concepts related to the field. The first fundamental concept of DEI is "diversity," which is typically defined as "the range of human differences, including but not limited to race, ethnicity, gender, sexual orientation, age, social class, physical ability or attributes, religious or ethical value system, national origin, and political beliefs" (NIH, 2017). In the United States, institutions often have a published definition of "diversity" on their website. The definitions used by universities and organizations in their institutional policies are quite similar to the previously quoted one. They are not exhaustive and never claim to be so, which is understandable because the lists of human characteristics and identities can never be complete. However, two issues around these definitions are noteworthy.

First, most "diversity" definitions do not consider an individual's language identity as being worthy of selection for this shortlist, and yet it is subjectively meaningful to many people. Language has an essential role in human existence. Not only does it allow us to share our thoughts and emotions, it is crucial for expressing and negotiating our identities. Moreover, language is an instrument of power. Second, these definitions reduce diversity within an institution to the presence or absence of representation of these differences. This can give the perception of disregarding the importance of one's lived experiences or overlooking intersectionality. For example, students from an ethnic majority can be automatically "put in the box" of being part of a privileged group. It can remain unnoticed that based on a variety of other aspects of their identity, such as their immigration status, accent or hidden disability, they have been discriminated against. The nuance that someone can have privileged and unprivileged identities simultaneously can often be lost in surface level diversity. This brings us to the discussion of the second fundamental concept of DEI, "equity."

"Equity" can be defined as "the state, quality, or ideal of being just, impartial, and fair" (Annie E. Casey Foundation, 2014, p. 5). It is important to distinguish "equity" from "equality," the term, which is widely used, for example, in the United Kingdom in the "EDI" acronym, standing for Equality, Diversity, and Inclusion. The difference between the two terms is that "equality" means providing people with "an equal opportunity to make the most of their lives and talents and that one person should not have an advantage over another 'because of the way they were born, where they are from, what they believe, or whether they have a disability' (Equality and Human Rights Commission, 2018)" (Lantz-Deaton & Golubeva, 2020, p. 178). Equality protects from discrimination as people are given "equal treatment." For instance, in the UK, under the Equality Act (2010), there are nine protected characteristics: (1) age, (2) disability, (3) gender reassignment, (4) marriage and civil partnership, (5) pregnancy and maternity, (6) race, (7) religion or belief, (8) sex, and (9) sexual orientation. While equality ensures that everyone gets the same opportunity, equity takes care of understanding what kind of support people need based on their individual, interpersonal and systemic context. Both equity and equality promote social justice, but the former involves structural changes and systemic efforts. From this point of view, equity is an aspiration and – whatever degree of detail an institution will be able to pay attention to – the situation can be improved but will never be fully equitable. An analogy commonly used to show the differences between the terms is that equality would be everyone receiving the exact same pair of shoes, therefore, getting equal treatment, while equity would be everyone receiving a pair of shoes that fit their body and mobility needs, therefore, having equal outcomes.

The third key concept is "inclusion," and it can be defined as "involvement and empowerment, where the inherent worth and dignity of all people is recognized" (NIH, 2017). While "diversity" can be described as numerical representation, "inclusion" involves active participation and a sense of belonging. The purpose of enhancing inclusivity is to make every member of the community (organization, university campus, etc.) feel they belong and have voice, regardless of their age, disability, ethno-racial identity, gender and sexual orientation, social status, religion or belief, language and immigration background, or any other dimensions of diversity. Of note: in this definition, inclusion calls for everyone to feel like they have a voice but does not suggest that all voices need to be in agreement for inclusion to exist.

Additionally, "social justice" is a concept that is fundamental for theoretical orientation of DEI and also serves as a practical ideal. Defined as "the fair treatment and equitable status of all individuals and social groups within a state or society," social justice refers to "social, political, and economic institutions, laws, or policies that collectively afford such fairness and equity and is commonly applied to movements that seek fairness, equity, inclusion, self-determination, or other goals for currently or historically oppressed, exploited, or marginalized populations" (Duignan, 2024, para. 1). Similarly to "DEI," due to its highly political and ideological nature, the notion of "social justice" has many other readings and interpretations and is often used in a narrower sense, depending on context and specific circumstances (see Duignan, 2024; Nussbaum, 1999, etc.). However, for this text I will use social justice in the previous meaning.

Another term central to this discussion is the "sense of belonging." While the four previously discussed – diversity, equity, inclusion, and social justice – can be observed, measured, or described through the state-of-practice at institutional level; the sense of belonging is subjective and can be defined as an individual's perception of campus inclusiveness and the feeling of psychological safety. The sense of belonging is important because it allows us to be ourselves and perform our best while actively participating in diverse communities. It can be developed if students perceive that they have support from their professors and peers (Hoffman et al., 2003). Ingram (2012) differentiated three categories of belonging: social, academic, and perceived institutional support. Greater peer relatability correlated with heightened reported social belonging among students. Furthermore, students who perceived the curriculum as personally relevant demonstrated higher scores across all three measures of belonging. In the InterEqual project reported in Section 4, enhancing social and academic belonging was a key focus.

The main challenge when trying to enhance students' sense of belonging in a systematic way at a university is the individual and subject nature of the term and how each student conceptualizes their university. For each student, a sense of belonging can have multiple meanings. Some students may prioritize social belonging because they need to feel valued members of the campus community. Others may seek academic belonging (i.e., supportive faculty and staff, and reliable study groups) or institutional support (i.e., specific student services and safety) (Golubeva, in press). Moreover, priorities may change over the course of students' studies at university. This can be explained through the lens of their lived experiences and the fluidity and hybridity of identities (Bhabha, 2006; Buckingham, 2008; Hall & Du Gay, 2006), which can swiftly shift as a result of interactions with campus members or a larger community. The fluid and dynamic nature of identity makes it difficult to categorize and classify individuals in a meaningful way, without stereotyping. This is why for the DEI field, to better understand how social identities overlap, it is important to more broadly incorporate intersectionality (Crenshaw, 1989, 1991).

While not long ago, most studies in the field of DEI focused on a single aspect of social identity (e.g., age, sex, race) in a domestic context, predominantly the workplace (Shore et al., 2009); today, DEI efforts strive to take into account the entire complexity of human experience and extend its understanding beyond purely demographic differences to include the intersectionality of identities, and overlapping systems of power and oppression. The term "intersectionality" was coined by Crenshaw (1989) and originally used to discuss the multidimensionality of Black women's experience and their treatment in antidiscrimination law, more specifically, how systems of oppression (racism and sexism) overlap. Today, this concept is often used in a broader meaning, acknowledging that various characteristics or social identities (e.g., ethnicity, race, language background, age, gender, sexual orientation, ideological views and religious beliefs, disabilities, and other dimensions of diversity) can intersect to further marginalize people, placing them at even greater disadvantages within systems of power. Conversely, the intersection of privileged characteristics can further enhance an individual's advantages within these systems. However, as Hoffart (2023) cautions, the concept of "intersectionality" is often misunderstood and, therefore, misused. Often intersectionality is simplified to an idea that someone is not just one aspect of their identity at any specific time without commenting on the overlapping systems. It appears to be one of the most controversial concepts in the research concerning the DEI issues. Hoffart refers to these debates as "intersectionality wars," noting that instead of providing answers and having "a unifying purpose," they rather create division (2023, p. 40). His opinion echoes Nash's, who points out that

> Nearly everything about intersectionality is disputed: its histories and origins, its methodologies, its efficacy, its politics, its relationship to identity and identity politics, its central metaphor, its juridical orientations, its relationship to "black woman" and to black feminism. (Nash, 2017, pp. 117–118)

With specific reference to feminist researchers (May, 2015; Tomlinson, 2018, etc.) and academic literature on intersectionality (Cho et al., 2013; Crenshaw, 1989, etc.), Hoffart (2023) centers his analysis around "intersectional intersectionality" and "additive intersectionality." "Additivity," as he explains, "denotes a way of conceptualising the relationship between different social categories or systems of oppression where these categories (like gender, race, class, sexuality) or systems (like sexism, racism, classism, heterosexism) are seen as separate and independent, which then makes it possible to add them to each other" (Hoffart, 2023, p. 48). In contrast to intersectional intersectionality, additive intersectionality views an individual as a simple combination of separate identities and not in intertwining ways. The difference between these opposing narratives and methodological approaches can be illustrated through the following two modes of thought (based on Hoffart, 2023, p. 52):

Intersectional ⟷ Additive
Non-essentialist ⟷ Essentialist
Nonbinary ⟷ Binary
Inclusive ⟷ Exclusionary
Fluid ⟷ Solid
Dynamic ⟷ Static
Becoming ⟷ Finished
Experience-near ⟷ Experience-far
Dialogic ⟷ Monologic
(Self-)reflective ⟷ (Power-)blind

The intersectional intersectionality approach shows a clear relevance to the mindset of intercultural citizenship. Additive thinking is not compatible with intersectional thinking (Bowleg, 2008, p. 314) as it is not compatible with the intercultural citizenship education approach.

Before we move to a brief overview of the history of the DEI field, it is important to acknowledge, first, that there exist numerous other concepts relevant to DEI work, such as identity development, accessibility, and accountability. However, due to length limitations, I will not be able to include them all. Second, and more importantly, the terminology of the field of DEI was coined in the Anglo-Saxon context, which can be problematic and cause tensions in other local contexts (and languages). For example, the previously discussed concept of "intersectionality" was theorized and thematized in the US context, which holds a potential risk of "reproducing the US-centric structure of the field" outside of its "home," "universalized as a non-context, a non-location" (see Hoffart, 2023, p. 33). Therefore, before we continue, please take a moment to reflect on Thought Box 6.

THOUGHT BOX 6 REFLECTING ON DISMANTLING ESSENTIALIST PERSPECTIVES IN DEI WORK AND ICITE AND CENTERING UNDERREPRESENTED AND MARGINALIZED VOICES

▶ Although having a well-defined, robust theory is undoubtedly helpful in the research and practice, how can we guarantee that underrepresented and marginalized voices receive attention in academic discourse?

THOUGHT BOX 6 (cont.)

▶ When a particular theoretical framework gains prominence and is endorsed through cultural and political narratives in mainstream media, how can we prevent the exclusion or marginalization of certain viewpoints, perspectives, and/or lived experiences?

Please note that there are no definitive answers to these queries. However, ongoing introspection and (self-)reflection can aid in dismantling an essentialist perspective within the realms of DEI work and ICitE.

In the United States, the history of DEI traces back to the civil rights movement and major changes in the legal system aimed at eradicating the enduring impacts of slavery, racism and white supremacy. In the 1960s–70s, the main focus was on anti-discrimination legislation to rectify prior laws and policies that were explicitly racist. Historical landmarks such as *Brown v. Board of Education* in 1954 (Warren, 1954) and the Civil Rights Act of 1964 (*Title VII*, 1964) were important in ensuring equal access to education and addressing disparities in healthcare, criminal justice, and other aspects of social life. Prior to the 1960s there was little racial, economic, or gender diversity in HE in the United States (outside of Historically Black Colleges and Universities (HBCUs) and other minority-serving institutions (MSIs[12]) that were traditionally and intentionally underfunded). Civil rights movements, advocating for justice and equality for Black Americans, were bolstered by student and faculty activism and mass protests across the nation. Universities served as a hub for progressive thought, social change, and education of democratic values and human rights (see, e.g., Online Exhibits at the University of Michigan Library, n.d.). Since then, hundreds of academic departments and programs in Black and African American studies have been launched in the United States. In the 1970s, the corporate world started practicing affirmative action: at the beginning, when doing recruitment, and later shifting to retention and promotion of minorities and women.

The next significant step in DEI work was the introduction of sensitivity and awareness training in the 1980s–90s, aimed to identify personal biases. The focus of these training sessions would vary depending on the local context. For example, in Australia, the primary aim was to address the historical discrimination against Aboriginal and Torres Strait Islander peoples (Vaughn, 2007). In

---

[12] In the United States, Minority Serving Institutions (MSIs) are colleges and universities created to increase access to HE for underserved minorities (see more on MSI Program here: www.doi.gov/pmb/eeo/doi-minority-serving-institutions-program).

many places in Asia, the DEI work addressed the long-standing tensions between Muslim and Hindu communities. In South Africa, diversity education aimed at helping the dismantling of the Apartheid system. And, in many European countries, it was focused on fighting xenophobic attitudes due to increased migration. In the United States, the focus was mainly on racism initially, and later, gender diversity sensitization and tolerance toward religious and LGBTQ+ communities were added. These DEI efforts contributed to more positive attitude toward gays and lesbians, which was especially negative among historically dominant religious communities (Vaughn, 2007 referring to Devine & Monteith, 1993).

Increasing globalization and workplace diversity created an increased demand to broaden the scope of DEI training in response to rising multiculturalism, which refers to "the inclusion of the full range of identity groups in education" (Vaughn, 2007). Vaughn (2007) reports that at the same time universities in the United States started offering diversity courses that students could use to fulfill general education requirements. However, at the beginning of 1980s, compulsory DEI education was met with similar resistance in HE as in other sectors (industry, corporate world, military, etc.) (Day, 1983). During this decade the number of training programs was growing, which led to the professionalization of the field and the emergence of Chief Diversity Officer positions.

Over time, cultural context changed resulting in less resistance to DEI initiatives. In the 2000s, the attention of the field expanded to an even broader variety of identity aspects, which included disabilities and sexual orientation. The number of DEI-focused positions continued to grow, and a new (more instrumental) aspect was added that viewed diversity as an opportunity to attract "the best and the brightest" to universities and workplaces. In the context of US higher education, this resulted in a rapid expansion of student enrollment in colleges and universities and recruitment of faculty and staff from underrepresented minorities, but, unfortunately, less has been achieved in terms of building inclusive campuses. The proportion of white students in 1976 accounted[13] for 83% of all college students; by 2016 they accounted for 57% of all college students due to policies like affirmative action at elite institutions, increased financial aid, the expansion of community colleges, and other social factors. During that same time, the proportion of college students who are Black or Hispanic increased from 10% to 14% and from 4% to 18%, respectively (Menand, 2020).

---

[13] Of note, there are shortcomings in DEI statistics; therefore, they should be reviewed with care. Quite often, for example, the reports do not include data on Indigenous, Native American, and Pacific Islanders. Also, students from the Middle East and North Africa (MENA) region are automatically added to the "White students" category.

While the demographic statistics demonstrated significant progress in terms of diversity, the retention rates of underrepresented minorities members showed less prominent improvement. Vaughn (2007 referring to Fenn & Irvin, 2005) described this attitude as "let's just get as many students of color in as possible and worry about how to retain them later."

The past decade has been characterized by (1) the raise of social movements (e.g., like #BlackLivesMatter, #MeToo, and #StopAAPIHate), and (2) a stronger focus on compliance with Federal regulations, which included obligatory training as, for example, the Title IX training at US universities (see also Section 2.2). The main goal of these training initiatives is to inform students, faculty, and staff about the policies for mandated reporting, but they do not necessarily prevent or stop discrimination and sexual harassment. Of note, the focus on compliance can be tied to the politics of how US universities (both private and public) are funded by state and federal governments.

Although over the years, thanks to DEI efforts, there has been progress, the goals of DEI efforts are not complete. It can be stated with certainty that neither job promotion opportunities nor salaries are equal, and work still must be done. For example, in the United States, while women earn 59% of master's degrees (NCES, 2017) and form 52.8% of the college-educated workforce (U.S. Bureau of Labor Statistics, 2023), only 4.8% of CEOs in 500 largest companies are women (Zarya, 2018). Similarly low is women's, and in particular women's of color, representation in leadership positions in industries such as film and television production, medicine, high-tech industry, and politics (for detailed overview see Warner et al., 2018). In 2023, women comprised only 25% of the US Senate and 29% of the US House of Representatives (Center for American Women in Politics, 2023; Quorum, 2023). Although in the past decade the majority of doctorate (PhD) degrees in the United States have been earned by women, only 32% of full professors and 30% of college presidents are women (Warner et al., 2018). The wage gap between men and women, although narrower than it was in the 1970s, is still significant, with full-time women professors earning 82% of what their male colleagues earn (Carlton, 2023), while taking on their shoulders on average 1.4 more service workload per academic year as their male colleagues. For full professors this average is even higher at 2.4 times more work (Guarino & Borden, 2017).

A similar pay gap exists in the European context, with women earning on average 16.2% less than men (EC, 2018b). Among the European Union member states, the largest gap was observed in Estonia (25.3%) (EC, 2018b). In Europe, as in the United States, women are offered fewer opportunities for promotion and less generous bonuses, despite the fact that significantly more (10.8% more) women than men have completed higher education degrees (Eurostat, 2022). To combat this, several measures have been introduced in order to establish pay transparency. In Germany, the *Act to Promote Transparency in Wage Structures* (*Entgelttransparenzgesetz*) came into force in 2017. In Poland, a free Internet application was launched to measure the pay gap between women and men in both private and public sectors, and in the United Kingdom, companies with over 250 employees are required to report the gender pay gap data (see for further details EC, 2018b). Ironically, even among DEI professionals the issue of diversity and equity remains unresolved (see, e.g., Barger, 2023; Nwanji, 2023).

While diversity policies, training, and other initiatives are well intentioned, there are a number of concerns in their regard. Studies suggest that they may send wrong signals developing an illusionary belief in individuals that their organization/institution is fair, while they overlook cases of discrimination and sexual harassment (Dover et al., 2014; Kaiser et al., 2013). According to Lipman's (2018) estimation, US companies spend around 8 billion dollars on DEI training programs. However, their effectiveness proves to be limited, and often "one-size-fits-all" training sessions do not bring the desired results (Onyeador et al., 2021). The lack of effectiveness of these training initiatives should not be viewed as an indication that the values of DEI are not important but, instead, I believe, point to pedagogical challenges. To give a simple example, it would be unrealistic to expect limited training or education on a subject like addition to sufficiently prepare a student to do multiplication. Instead, a systematic and scaffolded approach is used to build mathematical competence. This is why I strongly believe that DEI should be incorporated in HE curricula across disciplines. This would aid in building a culture of mutual respect and enhance intercultural dialogue by bringing together diverse perspectives and approaches to problem-solving and by learning to collaborate across differences and allow for an approach that is mindful of where students are at developmentally. This is where DEI and ICitE can complement each other, which I will expand on in the next section.

3.4 The Intersections of DEI and ICitE

Section 3.4 summarizes significant points of intersection between DEI work and Intercultural Citizenship Education, along which the two can be synergized. I illustrate this by presenting a model (see Figure 2) that outlines some key common attributes of DEI and ICitE, and discuss ways for synergizing them in a mutually beneficial manner.

As discussed in Sections 3.2 and 3.3, the two fields have distinct histories and disciplinary roots. In terms of theoretical foundations, they typically refer to different corpora of research literature, and their primary focus differs as well.

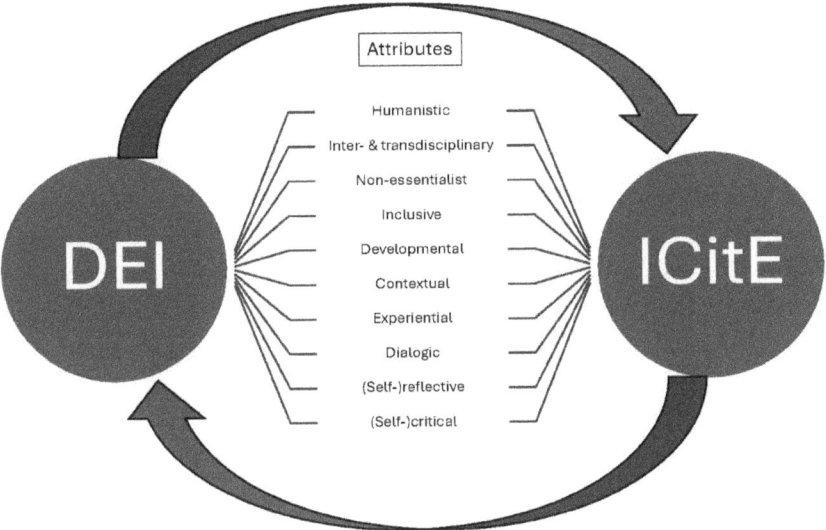

Figure 2 Synergies between DEI and ICitE.

However, despite the observed difference in perspectives between Intercultural Citizenship Education and DEI work, I argue that the two fields can complement each other in various positive and productive ways, particularly in their effort to promote inclusion and foster empathy and understanding between people coming from diverse backgrounds. Instead of listing some common values, goals, and practices shared by these two fields, I propose some key attributes that illustrate the intersections between DEI and ICitE. I do this intentionally because every model is inherently a simplification and may, therefore, have a limiting effect on one's understanding of the complexity of these phenomena, while my purpose is to offer a flexible, open-ended understanding of potential synergies between DEI and ICitE, adaptable to a variety of contexts. To this end, I describe the intersections using adjectives rather than nouns, which I view as a more dynamic and less rigid way to define the evolving fields such as DEI and ICitE.

This is a nonexhaustive attribute list: it highlights some key characteristics that should ideally be present in both DEI and ICitE theories and practices. These attributes are: (1) humanistic, (2) inter- and transdisciplinary, (3) non-essentialist, (4) inclusive, (5) developmental (along a continuum), (6) contextual, (7) experiential, (8) dialogic, (9) (self-)reflective, and (10) (self-)critical.

Humanistic: First and foremost, both DEI and ICitE serve the purpose of advancing the humanistic agenda of HE, that is, to prepare students for life and work in culturally diverse communities (see Section 1.3 for discussion). This shared goal emphasizes the development of values, attitudes, skills, knowledge and critical understanding that are necessary in an increasingly interconnected world. At the core of the humanistic agenda is the recognition that HE has a responsibility to prepare students for navigating complex social and cultural landscapes. DEI initiatives focus on creating inclusive environments that appreciate diversity and promote social justice; while ICitE facilitates the development of competencies necessary for one to become an active, interculturally and democratically competent, and global-minded citizen. By synergizing the efforts, DEI and ICitE can help students to move beyond passive awareness of diversity. They encourage meaningful interaction across cultural differences based on mutual respect, enabling students to actively contribute to the well-being of diverse communities. However, this can work only if HE is viewed in a given country/state/institution as a "public good." Otherwise, when the focus is shifted toward more individualistic, market-driven goals, such as economic competitiveness, the broader societal role of education in fostering inclusion, social justice, intercultural understanding, and active citizenship may be disregarded, or reduced to tokenism and compliance-based initiatives, rather than preparing students for life and work in diverse communities.

Inter- and Transdisciplinary: Both DEI and ICitE are inter- and transdisciplinary, meaning they should by definition be epistemologically open to new knowledge and diverse perspectives, inviting critique, and seeking new ways for implementing their goals across a variety of disciplines. Furthermore, both fields should strive to include underrepresented voices. Given that research on DEI and ICitE is rooted in Western academia and predominantly published in the English language, researchers from other epistemic traditions remain marginalized and unheard. A joint effort in decentering and decolonizing the research and practice could result in both scientific and social benefits.

Non-essentialist: The two fields seek to raise students' awareness of the significance of human diversity. However, there is a risk of essentializing based on certain identities if DEI and ICitE are not implemented with care and critical reflection. Both fields have been criticized for reducing complex, multifaceted identities to oversimplified categories, which can inadvertently reinforce stereotypes and neglect human experiences. In the context of DEI, essentializing might occur if diversity is approached as a checkbox of predetermined categories: "It entails the tendency to understand social categories as expressions of discrete, fixed, natural, uniform, and defining characteristics that are shared by all members, and are informative about them" (Soylu Yalcinkaya et al., 2017, p. 1). Similarly, in ICitE, there is a risk of reducing cultural identities to such traits as nationality or first language (see also Holliday, 2011). To fully capture the richness of individual identities, both fields should adopt a nuanced, non-essentialist approach that acknowledges the multifaceted, dynamic, fluid, and hybrid nature of identities and avoids predetermined categories, presuming that "all members of Group X think and behave the same way."

Inclusive: The fourth attribute is closely related to the previous one (non-essentialist), as both recognize diversity and uniqueness of human identities. The two fields, DEI and ICitE, emphasize creating inclusive environments where diverse perspectives and identities are valued and integrated. However, there is a nuanced difference in how they approach these goals with the former being concerned with intergroup power dynamics and the latter seeking to improve interpersonal communication. Combining these two would be mutually beneficial. On one hand, this would help DEI to address the critiques that it promotes essentialist thinking and narrative of "us" vs "them," when members of "other" groups are placed into preconceived "boxes," and the complex intersectionality of their identities can be oversimplified. On the other hand, it would help the field of Intercultural Citizenship Education, which tends to focus on competences an individual needs to communicate and interact across cultural differences, to adopt DEI's focus on "co-creating" culture by nurturing belonging, advancing equity, enhancing inclusion, and promoting social justice as well as its attention to systems and power.

Developmental: Another attribute concerns the developmental nature of DEI and ICitE, especially in terms of learning process and outcomes. DEI could adopt from ICitE's methodological approach of viewing students as being on a continuum and scaffolding their developmental process (e.g., from "racist" to "not racist" – see Helms, 1995). This could address the perception that DEI training initiatives often fail to meet students where they are at developmentally and potentially reduce negative experiences that put students on the defensive. Numerous models in intercultural education could be used for this purpose. See, for example, Bennett's Intercultural Development Model (Bennett, 1993), or three-level scaled descriptors of the Reference Framework of Competences for Democratic Culture (CoE, 2018). The latter is in particular suitable and can serve as a bridging framework for synergizing DEI and ICitE because it is based on the values shared by both fields, has a strong focus on democratic and intercultural competences, and is applicable to many countries and cultures (please refer to Section 3.2 and CoE, 2018 to learn more about the RFCDC, and to Section 4 for practical application of this framework).

Contextual: DEI and Intercultural Citizenship Education are inherently contextual. They cannot be acontextual as they need to be adapted to the specific sociopolitical, (lingua)cultural, and historical circumstances of the regions where they are implemented. Not only issues, but their understanding and perception may significantly vary and are context-dependent (see, e.g., Crenshaw, 1991; DiAngelo, 2022; Hall, 1976; Lustig & Koester, 2010). Let us explore some practical examples of how the foci of DEI and ICitE may be tailored to specific needs. For example, in Germany, DEI priority might be addressing modern-day xenophobia and integrating large numbers of refugees from Syria and Ukraine. In Australia, DEI efforts might focus on the recognition of Aboriginal and Torres Strait Islander peoples' sovereignty. ICitE, in the context of Latin America, might address historical injustices stemming from colonialism, to recognize the cultural rights of Indigenous groups; and in the context of suffering from apartheid South Africa – on reconciliation and fostering social cohesion through education. In a multicultural urban environment, subject to increasing migration, such as Paris, France, ICitE may promote building intercultural dialogue for living peacefully among a wide array of ethnic, religious, linguistic, and cultural communities. Or, as another example, during the times of global COVID-19 pandemic, ICitE may focus on sensitizing students to issues of human suffering and engaging them in constructive civic/social action (see, e.g., the intercultural citizenship telecollaboration organized by Porto et al., 2023). This leads us to the next shared attribute.

Experiential: Both DEI and ICitE emphasize the importance of active engagement, which makes the pedagogical methods based on experiential learning (Passarelli & Kolb, 2012) effectively applicable in their approaches. DEI work is action-oriented, which is an orientation Intercultural Citizenship Education has been striving to achieve (see, e.g., Byram et al., 2017; Porto et al., 2023; Rauschert & Byram, 2018). There are multiple forms of engaging students in hands-on, real-world experiences, including, but not limited to, community-based projects, service learning, study abroad programs, and intercultural telecollaboration. For example, an opportunity to experience diversity and to understand the lived realities of people coming from distinct (lingua)cultural backgrounds is to participate in community-based learning with immigrants. Collaborating on global issues such as human rights, climate disasters, and Indigenous rights, with students from different countries/backgrounds can foster a sense of shared responsibility and global-mindedness. Engaging in real-world scenarios provides a powerful means to bridge the goals of DEI and ICitE. Experiential learning can serve as a catalyst for realizing these goals by offering authentic opportunities to observe how different dimensions of identity (gender, age, immigration status, (lingua)cultural background, socioeconomic class, etc.) intersect and what impact this has on people's lived experiences.

Dialogic: The eighth attribute is at the core of both DEI and ICitE practices. DEI initiatives often rely on intergroup dialogue to challenge unconscious bias; to critically explore issues that polarize society, and to stimulate social action (see, e.g., Dessel et al., 2006; Grenny et al., 2022; Gurin et al., 2011; Quaye & Harper, 2015). A multi-university study showed that intergroup dialogue can improve students' understanding of race, gender, and income inequality; increase their intergroup empathy and cognitive openness, as well as their engagement in post college social and political action (Gurin et al., 2011). Equally critical is dialogue in Intercultural Citizenship Education (see CoE, 2008; EP, 2015: Lundgren et al., 2020, etc.). Through intercultural dialogue people coming from different (lingua)cultural backgrounds share their diverse (sometimes conflicting) perspectives, negotiate meanings across divides, and resolve conflicts. Dialogue not only enhances a sense of belonging through relationship building but is a prerequisite for building democratic cultures. It is important to underscore that dialogue in both DEI and ICitE practices has transformative potential. This makes it a vital attribute in both fields.

(Self-)reflective and (Self-)critical: Two last but not least significant attributes emphasize the importance of such analytical thinking skills as self-reflection and self-criticality. The association of intercultural communication with critical cultural (self-)awareness and political education (see Byram, 2008, 2021) makes ICitE and the related models and frameworks particularly well suited for DEI. As Byram argues,

> in an educational framework which aims to develop *critical* cultural awareness, questioning of one's own and respecting others' meanings, beliefs, values and behaviours does not happen without a reflective and analytical challenge to the ways in which they have been formed and the complex of social forces within which they are experienced. (Byram, 2021, p. 46)

This strong emphasis on fostering (self-)reflection and (self-)criticality can be adopted by DEI as a pedagogical approach and serve as a guiding principle for identifying training needs. (Self-)reflection is essential for individuals to examine their own identities, and to recognize their unconscious biases and privileges; while (self-)criticality is crucial in assessing one's own and others' practices, and institutional policies; challenging ethnocentric and essentialist views; and examining power dynamics. Both are equally important for individual and societal transformation.

The intersections between DEI and ICitE can be synergized, for example, by the former securing institutional support (provided DEI itself is supported at a given institution), and the latter offering pedagogical solutions for more systematic (intentional) integration of DEI and Intercultural Citizenship Education in university curricula. A joint effort of DEI and ICitE in emphasizing the humanistic role of HE could help to introduce a more sustainable approach for institutions and both fields to reach their educational goals.

As stated at the beginning of this section, this model is not exhaustive. Its primary purpose is threefold: (1) to facilitate through simplification a deeper understanding of the emerging fields of DEI and ICitE; (2) to describe the intersections between DEI and ICitE that can potentially be synergized for mutual benefit of the two; (3) to establish a theoretical foundation upon which further inquiry and experimentation can occur. To conclude the discussion of the proposed model, I refer to a famous aphorism attributed to George E. P. Box (Box et al., 2009, p. 61):

> All models are approximations. Assumptions, whether implied or clearly stated, are never exactly true. *All models are wrong, but some models are useful.* So the question you need to ask is not "Is the model true?" (it never is) but "Is the model good enough for this particular application?

Section 4 offers an example of how DEI and ICitE can be synergized in the context of higher education.

4 An Example of Synergizing DEI and ICitE on a Minority-Serving Campus in the United States

4.1 Introduction

Research on the campus climate has been the focus of HE scholarship for decades (Hart & Fellabaum, 2008). Nevertheless, studies show that challenges around inequalities, discrimination, and sense of belonging still negatively affect students' academic performance and the interpersonal/intergroup relations on campus (Hurtado et al., 2012; Hurtado & Ruiz Alvarado, 2012).

In this section, I offer an example of how a Minority Serving Institution developed a systematic training that integrated DEI and ICitE concepts and attributes. This is not to highlight this particular training as the "only" or "right" way to synergize DEI and ICitE concepts, but rather to demonstrate how such an effort *can* be approached. I discuss the results of a recent campus-wide survey conducted at an MSI (Golubeva et al., forthcoming), involving 1,535 undergraduate and graduate students. The study explored students' experiences with diversity, equity, and inclusion on campus as these relate to various aspects of their identity, as well as students' sense of belonging to a multicultural university community. The survey also scrutinized students' perceptions of the importance of intercultural and democratic citizenship competences, as outlined in the *Reference Framework of Competences for Democratic Culture* (CoE, 2018).

The findings from the campus-wide survey study informed the development of five training modules, which were then piloted with more than 200 undergraduate students from diverse majors. The InterEqual training, rooted in the synergies between DEI and ICitE, serves as an exemplar of how this approach can be implemented in university practice. I conclude the section by presenting results from both qualitative and quantitative data and discussing the impact of participation in the InterEqual training on fostering a more inclusive university campus.

4.2 Insights from a Campus-Wide Survey

In the fall of 2021, my colleagues and I (Golubeva et al., forthcoming) conducted a campus-wide survey at an MSI in the Mid-Atlantic region of the United States. The fall 2021 semester in the United States involved a massive return to on-campus learning after many universities had shifted to online learning in the spring of 2020, in response to the height of the COVID-19 lockdown. Among other challenges, the pandemic exacerbated political polarization, economic inequalities, and social isolation and led to observed increases in mental health challenges among students. In the United States, this time was also marked with nationwide reactions, protests and unrest because of police brutality and systemic racism following the murder and deaths of unarmed Black individuals like George Floyd and Breonna Taylor. Therefore, the main objectives of our survey were (1) to explore students' perceptions of the campus climate and intergroup relations, (2) to identify which RFCDC competencies they would like to develop, and (3) to inform the design of training modules aimed at fostering campus inclusiveness.

Usually, campus climate surveys focus on specific aspects of a campus. Among the areas most scrutinized are topics like student services, institutional policies, classroom practices, accessibility of public spaces, and social life (Harper & Hurtado, 2007; Hart & Fellabaum, 2008, etc.). These assessments are typically conducted by Student Affairs, Institutional Research, or DEI Offices, and are designed specifically to inform internal practices or initiatives at the university. The main reasons for surveying the campus community include: (1) identifying concerns related to safety, well-being, infrastructure, and so on; (2) assessing diversity and inclusivity of the campus community; (3) gathering feedback on experiences related to studying, working, and living on campus; (4) gaining insight into specific issues for informed, data-driven decision-making; and (5) fostering trust by soliciting the opinions of community members. While the discussion of survey results often leads to a revision of existing or the introduction of new institutional policies and practices, the effectiveness of these changes is not easily measured, and therefore, students continue to be impacted by the negative issues identified through those surveys and new issues emerge on campuses as the student body changes faster than new policy and practices are developed.

Our campus climate survey (Golubeva et al., forthcoming) not only sought to diagnose the campus climate of an MSI but also sought to gain insights into areas that could benefit from campus-wide pedagogical interventions. To ensure the depth and breadth of our initiative, our project team comprised university faculty, students, staff, and administrative leadership from several departments and offices, and various disciplinary backgrounds. The reliability of the campus-wide survey was tested through a pilot with over 150 students, and its validity was assessed by a three-round Delphi panel of an interdisciplinary group of world-renowned experts in the fields of Psychology; Language and Intercultural Communication Education, and Assessment; Internationalization of HE; and DEI.

The survey contained three primary parts. We explored (1) students' experiences with diversity, equity, and inclusion on campus as these relate to various aspects of their identity, as well as (2) students' sense of belonging to a multicultural university community. Specifically, we scrutinized students' interpersonal/intergroup relations and on-campus friendships. Also, we surveyed students about (3) the values, attitudes, skills, knowledge and critical understanding, as outlined in the *Reference Framework of Competences for Democratic Culture* (CoE, 2018), to gather their perceptions of the importance of each area of competence; if they had been provided with opportunities to develop these intercultural and democratic citizenship competences while studying at the university; and what competences they were interested in developing further.

Next I offer a brief overview of the key findings from our campus-wide survey (Golubeva et al., forthcoming).

4.2.1 Students' Perceptions Regarding Diversity, Equity, and Inclusion

Overall, students overwhelmingly reported that the MSI is both diverse and inclusive and that diversity enhances their campus experience (see Figure 3). To the question of whether the university provides spaces in which students feel safe to discuss topics related to diversity, equity, and inclusion, the majority of respondents also answered positively (see Figure 3). However, when looking at the strength of student feelings, we found that students did not feel as strongly about campus inclusivity as they did about the other three questions. A closer look at the data shows that the proportion of students perceiving the campus as "very inclusive" was somewhat lower compared to the number of students who said the campus was "very diverse" (see Figure 4). The number of negative answers for all four questions was very low and varied between 1.70% and 5.02% for "somewhat disagree" and 0.29% and 2.18% for "disagree" (see Figure 4).

When asked about specific aspects of identities, the percentage of students who "agreed" or "somewhat agreed" that the MSI campus is inclusive of their

DEI and Intercultural Citizenship in Higher Education   49

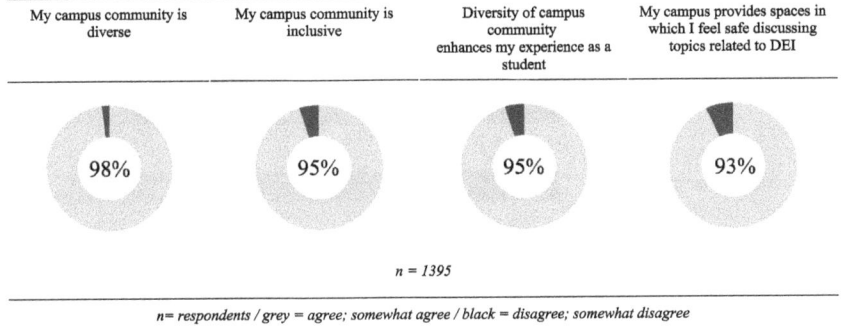

Figure 3 Level of agreement with statements related to diversity, equity, and inclusion.

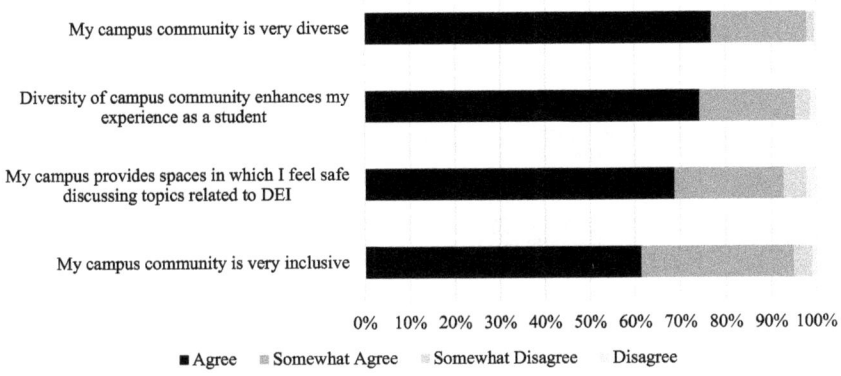

Figure 4 Students' general perceptions on campus diversity and inclusiveness (*n* = 1395).

ethno-racial identity, gender, sexual orientation, religious views, and spiritual beliefs, as well as their ideological/political worldviews, ranged between 90% and 97% (see Figure 5). Though the majority of students responded positively to all five questions, a comparison of the survey items revealed that the largest proportion of students who disagreed with the statement about campus inclusivity were those reporting perceptions related to their "ideological/political worldviews." (Of note, the survey did not ask students what their ideological/political worldviews were.) Responses related to perceiving campus as inclusive of their "religious views and spiritual beliefs" showed the next highest proportion of disagreement (see Figure 6). This, I believe, reflects the current state of social and political polarization, indicating an alarming level of intolerance toward diverse perspectives and opposing views.

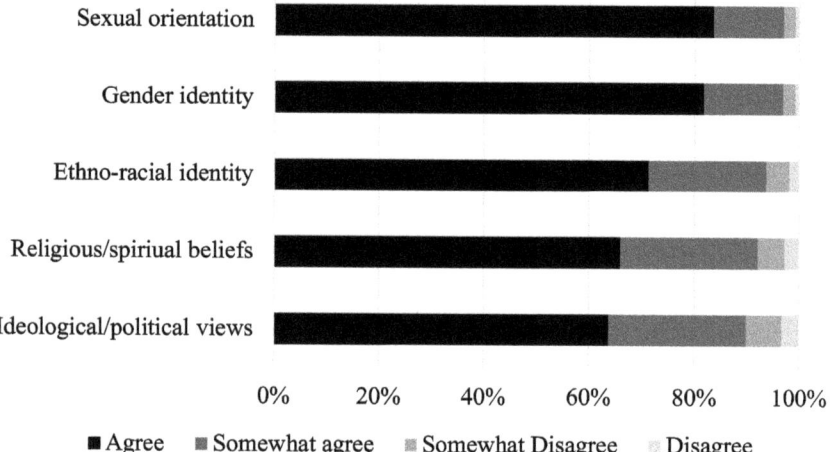

Figure 5 Level of agreement with statements related to specific aspects of the students' identity ($n = 937$).

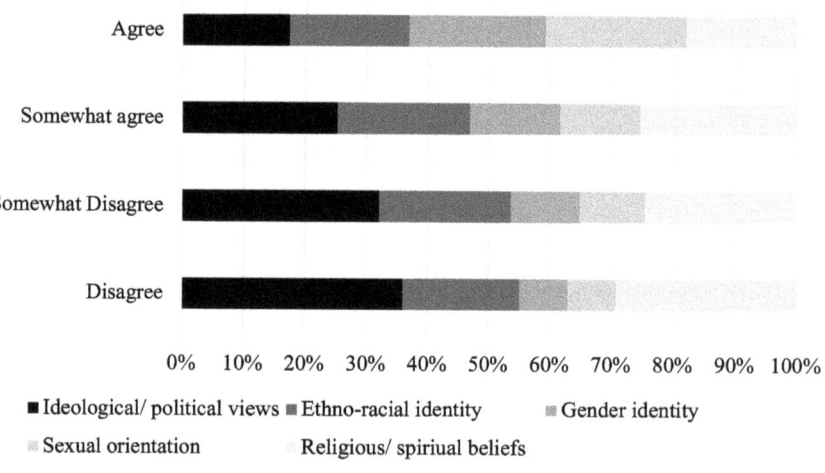

Figure 6 Level of agreement with statements related to specific aspects of the student's identity ($n = 937$) (100% stacker bar).

To the question "In which of the following spaces do you feel comfortable discussing topics related to diversity, equity, and inclusion?" the vast majority of respondents (82.77%) selected as their first choice – "with close friends," followed by "in face-to-face classrooms" (64.56%), "within student organizations" (52.45%) ($n = 917$). "With faculty" and "staff" only 41.55% and 33.81% of students, respectively, felt comfortable discussing topics related to DEI, while 3.27% of students preferred not to discuss these topics on campus at all.

The answers to the question "In which of the following spaces do you feel comfortable discussing topics related to your worldviews and beliefs?" demonstrated the same pattern. "With close friends" was ranked first by the majority of students (79.82%), followed by "in face-to-face classrooms" (59.43%), and "within student organizations" (48.84%) (*n* = 907). A notably lower proportion of students felt comfortable discussing worldviews and beliefs "with faculty" (38.15%) and "staff" (29.88%), and a significantly higher number of students (4.74%) preferred not to discuss this topic with anyone on campus.

We wanted to learn more about who the close friends were, more specifically, which aspects of identity the students shared with their friends. Based on the responses provided by 820 students, 90.61% of best friends spoke the same first language(s); 74.60% shared the same ethno-racial background, and 72.18% shared the same religious or spiritual beliefs.

4.2.2 Students' Perceptions of RFCDC Competences

As mentioned in the introduction to Section 4.2, the survey tool also included a series of questions based on the RFCDC model (CoE, 2018), consisting of a set of twenty values, attitudes, skills, knowledge and critical understanding areas connected to intercultural and democratic competences (see Figure 1). In particular, we sought to get information about which of these twenty areas the students perceive as the most important, which of them they felt the university already provided them with the opportunity to develop, and which of them they would like to develop further before they graduate.

When asked to rate the perceived level of importance of the RFCDC values, attitudes, skills, knowledge and critical understanding, the number of positive answers was very high, potentially indicating social desirability bias causing an overvaluation. However, despite this, the comparison of answers to all twenty items shows clear trends in students' perceptions.

In terms of values, *human dignity and human rights* were rated as being the most important (94.85%), followed by *democracy, justice, fairness, equality and the rule of law* (87.59%), and *cultural diversity* (84.66%) (*n* = 854). Among attitudes, *respect* (95.41%), *responsibility* (89.75%), *openness to cultural otherness and other beliefs, world views and practices* (86.57%), and *civic-mindedness* (80.80%) scored the highest. In terms of skills, *listening and observing* (89.68%), *analytical and critical thinking skills* (84.03%), *empathy* (83.31%), and *conflict-resolution skills* (82.59%). In the fourth set, *knowledge and critical understanding of the self* was rated as the most important (82.74%), followed by *knowledge & critical understanding of language and communication* (70.23%).

When the respondents were asked which area of competence the MSI had provided them with opportunities to develop, the least selected areas were:

- *conflict-resolution skills* (39.14%),
- *tolerance of ambiguity* (38.30%),
- *linguistic, communicative, and plurilingual skills* (40.10%),
- *knowledge and critical understanding of language and communication* (45.86%),
- *empathy* (46.34%),
- *civic-mindedness* (46.22%),
- *valuing democracy, justice, fairness, equality and the rule of law* (48.02%), and
- *knowledge and critical understanding of the self* (48.14%).

To identify campus training needs, the respondents were also asked to indicate which of twenty areas they would like to develop before graduating from the university. *Conflict-resolution skills* were selected the most, followed by *knowledge and critical understanding of the world (politics, law, human rights, culture, cultures, religions, history, media, economies, environment, sustainability)*; *analytical and critical thinking skills; linguistic, communicative and plurilingual skills; self-efficacy; knowledge and critical understanding of the self; listening and observing skills; flexibility and adaptability; autonomous learning skills; cooperation skills; knowledge and critical understanding of language and communication* (see Figure 7).

These findings informed the design of the intercultural training modules developed to build a more inclusive campus and improve students' sense of belonging to a culturally diverse campus at an MSI (see more on InterEqual in Section 4.3).

4.2.3 Differences in Perceptions between Mono- and Multilingual Students

While the theory and practice of ICitE– as discussed in this Element – is closely related to Foreign Language Education; DEI initiatives often lack attention to linguistic diversity in contrast to many other aspects of identity.[14] Hence, the objective of this section is to provide a research-based foundation for developing a more comprehensive and nuanced approach to DEI work, through examining the advantages of multilingualism. It is

---

[14] For example, in a 658-page anthology on diversity and social justice, out of 137 papers, 92 discuss the topics related to racism, 77 – sexism, 64 – classism, 39 – ableism, 35 – heterosexism, 17 – transgender oppression, 33 – ageism and adultism, 27 – religious oppression, 24 – global issues, and only 12 – language issues, including use of American Sign Language (Adams et al., 2013, pp. xv–xxii).

DEI and Intercultural Citizenship in Higher Education 53

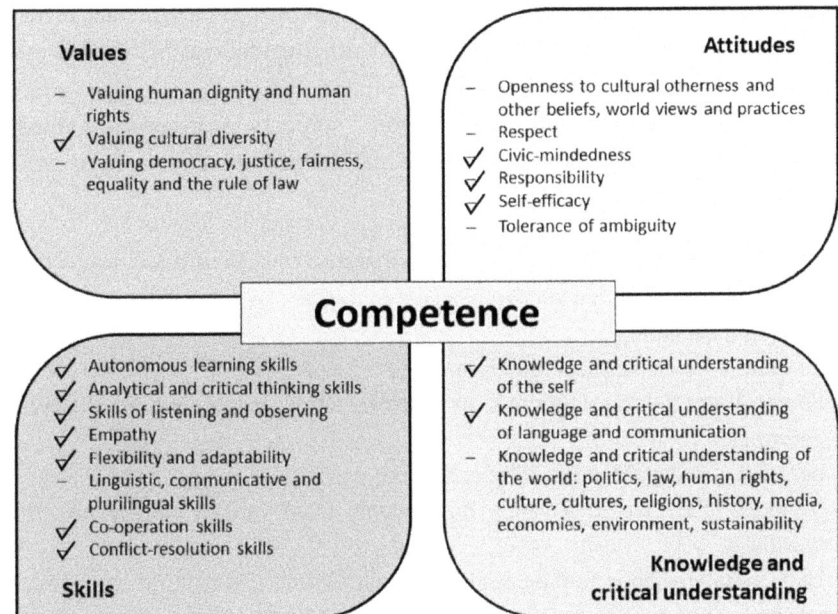

Figure 7 The RFCDC competences identified as major gaps/training needs (marked with checkmarks)

Source: CoE, 2018, Volume 1, p. 38. © Council of Europe, reproduced with permission; checkmarks added to indicate top areas students wanted to develop before graduation

important to note that the university where the survey was conducted has a language requirement. This means that undergraduate students are required to complete studies in a language other than English and reach the 201-level proficiency, the "Novice High" level, according to the classification proposed by the American Council for the Teaching of Foreign Languages (ACTFL) that can be compared to the "A2" level in the Common European Framework of Reference (CEFR).[15]

The participants of the campus-wide survey were asked to self-report their language knowledge. Out of 816 students who answered this question, 45.71% spoke one language, 35.91% spoke two, 14.46% – three, and 3.92% – four or more languages. In this section, I summarize the findings gained specifically from the undergraduate students' data ($n = 435$). To understand the perceptions that mono- and multilingual students had of campus, the responses collected from those who self-reported speaking two, three, four, or more languages were combined, and compared to the responses

---

[15] See the comparison of language proficiency levels according to ACTFL vs. CEFR: Framework Standards here: www.academiatica.com/actfl-vs-cefr-framework-standards-comparison/.

of those who spoke only one language. We found several significant differences between mono- and multilingual students when they were asked to rate how much a statement was "like them."

First and foremost, the multilingual students self-reported more frequently than their monolingual peers that the following statements were "like them":

- take the perspective of others; imagine themselves in their place, empathize with them, and look at everybody's side in the case of a disagreement before making a decision;
- be more adept to unusual situations;
- demonstrate a higher interest in learning how people live in different countries;
- be more curious about the religions of the world;
- be more interested in learning how people from various cultures see the world;
- be more interested in finding out about the traditions and cultural practices of various communities.

Furthermore, students who spoke multiple languages self-reported that they were more likely to respect value systems different from their own. When talking in their first language to people whose native language was different, a larger proportion of multilingual students reported that they carefully observe the reactions of their interlocutors; frequently check to make sure that they are understanding each other correctly, and are more careful when explaining things.

At the same time, speakers of two, or more languages were more critical of the university regarding diversity and inclusion:[16]

- A significantly larger proportion of multilinguals perceived their campus as being less diverse and less inclusive than their monolingual peers;
- In particular, multilingual students perceived the university being less inclusive of their ethno-racial identity, gender orientation, and religious/spiritual beliefs.

Finally, when looking at RFCDC competence areas, a significantly larger proportion of multilingual students ($p\text{-value} \leq 0.05$) rated the following values, attitudes, skills, knowledge and critical understanding areas as "very important" compared to their monolingual peers:

---

[16] These findings were statistically significant with *p-value* ≤ *0.05*.

Values:
- Valuing cultural diversity

Attitudes:
- Openness to cultural otherness and to other beliefs, worldviews and cultural practice
- Civic-mindedness
- Tolerance of ambiguity

Skills:
- Autonomous learning skills
- Skills of listening and observing
- Empathy

Knowledge and Critical Understanding areas:
- Knowledge and Critical Understanding of language and communication

When asked which of the RFCDC competences the students would want to develop further while studying at the university, significantly more multilinguals than monolinguals ($p\text{-}value \leq 0.05$) mentioned:

- Valuing human dignity and human rights;
- Valuing democracy, justice, fairness, equality and the rule of law;
- Knowledge and critical understanding of language and communication; and
- Knowledge and critical understanding of the world: politics, law, human rights, culture, cultures, religions, history, media, economies, environment, and sustainability.

In comparison to their monolingual peers, a significantly larger proportion of multilingual students ($p\text{-}value \leq 0.05$) saw an increased leadership opportunity as a benefit of developing intercultural and democratic competences.

Students with the ability to communicate in more than one language, negotiate meanings with interlocutors who speak other first language(s), come from different cultures, and do not share the same values and beliefs, indicated having more competence through their increased levels of critical thinking skills; empathy (including ability and willingness to take the perspective of others, and mediate in the situations of disagreement); tolerance of ambiguity; adeptness in handling unusual situations; observation and communication skills; curiosity and interest in learning about other cultural practices and belief systems. The results are consistent with a large body of research findings regarding the beneficial effects of bilingualism and multilingualism, and suggest that learning language(s) could contribute to building more inclusive campus communities.

The main implication of these findings is that DEI efforts should give more consideration to linguistic diversity and language education, as these hold strong potential in fostering competences requisite for an inclusive campus. The attributes discussed previously possess invaluable relevance in the super-diverse and dynamically evolving global landscape and more research should be conducted to explore if learning multiple languages has a causal relationship with these attributes. Therefore, it is lugubrious and unwise that the university administrators, including, in particular, those who (pretend to) advocate for diversity, equity, and inclusion, to overlook the value of language learning and cut language programs (see, e.g., Hanlon, 2023; Kingson, 2023, and many other cases across the United States and beyond). Such an approach is a clear example of pushing forward the instrumental agenda in HE while totally neglecting the role and benefits of humanities.

4.3 The InterEqual Training Modules

Section 4.3 presents an example of how Intercultural Citizenship Education and DEI can be synergized in HE settings, in the form of a training program. As stated earlier, this example is not intended to show the "only" or "right" way, but rather it is offered to demonstrate a possible approach to synergizing the two fields. The InterEqual training modules were designed to provide a unique and novel approach to teaching intercultural communication to university students at an MSI in the Mid-Atlantic region of the United States. The emphasis on developing competences related to democratic culture and intercultural citizenship suggests a focus not only on communication skills but also on fostering values that promote openness to diverse perspectives, inclusivity and equity.

4.3.1 Training Development

The development of the InterEqual training program began with a thorough self-evaluation of the university's intercultural and DEI programming, followed by a campus-wide survey to understand student perceptions. To ensure the depth and breadth of our initiative, our project team consisted of university faculty, students, staff, and administrative leadership from multiple departments and offices. This diversity of the research team was critical for the success of the project, and team members contributed in varied ways based on their expertise and time dedication.

Using the results from the campus-wide survey discussed in Section 4.2 allowed us to develop a tailored approach to address the specific needs of the diverse student community at the MSI. At the time of the survey, the student body at the MSI had both domestic and international diversity, with almost 9% of the students being international. Regarding ethno-racial diversity, the domestic student body was: 20% Black or African American, 19% Asian American, 16% Hispanic, 31% White, and approximately 5% other, including students of two or more races, Native Hawaiian or Other Pacific Islanders, American Indian or Alaska Native, and those who did not report their race. The InterEqual training is rooted in an inclusive approach that reflects this intra-institutional diversity and is founded on the recognition that one of the roles of HE is to prepare students "to interact with people from other (lingua)cultures in a multicultural community, both locally and globally, in a democratic and interculturally competent way" (Golubeva, 2022, pp. 191–192).

The work on the InterEqual training utilized the ADDIE model (Branson, 1978 referring to Branson et al., 1975), a well-established procedure for instructional systems development which is widely recognized among training developers and instructional designers. The acronym stands for Analyze, Design, Develop, Implement, and Evaluate, and this sequence proved to be effective in our project.

In phase 1, the *analysis phase,* the project team

– completed the institution's self-evaluation in terms of intercultural and DEI programming;
– conducted a campus-wide survey to learn about students and their perceptions and experiences of campus life, and
– analyzed the major gaps in terms of intercultural citizenship education.

In phase 2, the *design phase*, we determined the:

– content scope,
– training objectives/outcomes,
– learning strategies,
– assessment methods, and
– activity types.

During this phase, we utilized the Reference Framework of Competences for Democratic Culture (CoE, 2018), as our theoretical approach. Specifically, we focused on the values, attitudes, skills, knowledge and critical understanding areas that were identified as major gaps through the campus-wide survey. We adopted Holliday's (2011) *non-essentialist approach* and Barnett's (1997) *theory of criticality* in the development of intercultural and democratic citizenship competencies.

For assessment purposes, we employed both qualitative and quantitative methods, incorporating self-assessments like e-portfolios, pre- and post-surveys, as well as validated empathy and intercultural assessments, such as the Interpersonal Reactivity Index (Davis, 1980), the Toronto Empathy Questionnaire (Spreng et al., 2009), among others. The latter were utilized only during the pilot stage to evaluate the effectiveness of the training outcomes.

In phase 3, the *development phase*, we created the five modules and adopted them for an e-learning environment. Each module was scaffolded and consisted of a series of activities that we call "Steps." Our Steps are focused on (1) developing self-awareness, (2) critical thinking, and (3) empathy, through a variety of different activities including completing online discussion forums, lecturettes, reading and video activities, critical self-reflections, case studies, critical cultural incidents, simulations, self-assessments, e-portfolios, and small group projects. These activities were selected because of their alignment to our chosen theoretical orientations and the methodological approaches grounded in the work of Byram and colleagues on intercultural learning and citizenship education (Byram, 1997, 2008; Byram et al., 2017; Byram et al., 2021; Porto et al., 2023); Bloom and colleagues on learning strategies and assessment methods taxonomy (Anderson & Krathwohl, 2001; Bloom, 1956); Kolb (1984) on the experiential learning cycle; Gibbs (1988) on the reflective learning cycle; and Golubeva and Guntersdorfer (2020) on developing empathy. Additionally, we incentivize students who complete the InterEqual modules by introducing digital badges that can be added to students' LinkedIn profiles or included on their resume/CV.

In phase 4, the *implementation phase*, (1) we developed the procedures to pilot the modules, (2) prepared the instructors, and (3) recruited 200 undergraduate students across various majors to participate in the pilot. During the pilot, student progress was monitored, and feedback was collected on a weekly basis. At the end of the pilot semester, students were awarded module-level badges for each completed module, and a meta-badge if they completed all five.

Finally, in phase 5, the *evaluation phase*, we utilized Kirkpatrick's model (Kirkpatrick & Kirkpatrick, 2006), which consisted of an evaluation of (1) training participants' reaction, that is, whether they found the training relevant, engaging, and useful; (2) learning, that is, whether the students developed intended values, attitudes, skills, knowledge and critical understanding during training; (3) behavior, that is, whether students applied these competences during the training, for example, when collaborating on a joint project; and (4) results, that is, whether the outcomes demonstrate the impact of the training.

Of note, the first three phases of the project were extremely time intensive and covered the span of two academic years with half of that time being committed to the first stage. While not every institution will be able to devote such resources, our careful planning was critical for the success of the project. I will expand on this point more in my reflections (see Section 4.4.3).

4.3.2 Training Framework and Activities

The idea of the InterEqual training is rooted in the synergies between Diversity, Equity, and Inclusion efforts and Intercultural Citizenship Education. (For the theoretical underpinnings of the approach taken in the training, please refer to Section 3 in this Element.) The training activities were designed to help increase students' perception of campus inclusiveness and to enhance their sense of belonging in terms of diverse attributes of their identities, such as ethnicities, races, language and immigration backgrounds, ages, genders, sexual orientations, ideological views and religious beliefs, disabilities, and other demographic factors. We sought to create a safe environment where students can communicate on sensitive topics related to diversity, equity, inclusion, and social justice, by fostering meaningful discussions and collaboration with others, and through practicing critical self-reflection and empathy.

The pedagogical intervention's commitment to promoting fairness and equality, human dignity, and cultural diversity is reflected in the training title – InterEqual. The first part of the acronym – INTER – reflects its linkage with "intercultural" and refers to the titles of the five training modules:

I – Increasing Cultural Self-Awareness
N – Navigating Personal Bias
T – Transforming Communication and Building Collaboration across Cultural Differences
E – Exploring Inclusive Solutions to Intercultural Conflicts
R – Reinforcing Intercultural Dialogue

There are many topics that can be studied in the intercultural communication classroom. How and why did we decide on these five? We used the results from the campus-wide survey to tailor the InterEqual training to the specific needs of the diverse campus. To select the five modules content, we identified the major gaps in students' competences. For example, the module on "Exploring Inclusive Solutions to Intercultural Conflicts" was developed to respond to conflict-resolution skills being the most selected competence students wanted to develop before graduation (see survey findings in Section 4.2.2). In the case of other institutions, the selected topics may differ. It is important to note that training for institutions (and even the same institution over time) should be context-specific. For instance, at some institutions, there may be a greater need for training on xenophobia or culture shock.

The second part of the acronym – EQUAL – reflects its interrelationship with DEI efforts and refers to the methods applied in the training where participants are asked to:

E –   Engage
Q –   Question
U –   Understand
A –   Analyze and Act
L –   Listen and Learn

The EQUAL acronym encapsulates our methodological approach, where students learn from real-world experiences by engaging in meaningful communication, questioning assumptions, understanding diverse perspectives, analyzing situations, taking intentional actions, and practicing active listening. Such an approach fosters critical cultural self-awareness, empathy, and critical thinking while taking into account all four learning styles, as outlined in Kolb's model (1984), that is, *diverging, assimilating, converging,* and *accommodating* through engaging students in *concrete experience, reflective observation, abstract conceptualization,* and active *experimentation.*

To scaffold students' learning, the order of the InterEqual module-level learning objectives was carefully planned, following the revised version (Anderson & Krathwohl, 2001) of Bloom's taxonomy (Bloom, 1956) that involves such thinking processes as *remembering, understanding, applying, analyzing, evaluating,* and *creating.* The selection of the elements of the EQUAL acronym – engaging, questioning, understanding, analyzing and acting, and listening and learning – covers a wide range of cognitive processes along the continuum outlined in Bloom's taxonomy, and is meant to satisfy students' training needs in terms of skills (for reference, see 4.2.2).

The five content components (INTER) and the five methodological strategies (EQUAL) are interconnected, as illustrated in the InterEqual logo (see Figure 8). The logo also symbolizes that students learn through collaboration, from each other.

Figure 8 The InterEqual Framework (the badge logo designed by Collin Sullivan and Petra Janka at UMBC in 2022; reproduced with permission).

When designing our activities, we wanted to be as inclusive as possible. We did so by including situations that relate to their everyday lives, names that they hear in their classrooms, and topics that matter to them. When students see themselves represented in the curriculum, they engage in discussions because they feel that they belong and have a voice. This can be as simple as reflecting the diversity of their names. We can reflect the (lingua)cultural diversity of the student body by not only using names like Bill, John, Mary or Ann. In the case of my institution, using names like Ali, Katha, Fatema, Aditya, David, Petra, Natalia, Praveen, Kevin, Eun, Versana, Daniel, Chang, Aron, Juan, Rachel, Adelheid, Oksana, and Adebayo more accurately reflects the diverse student body. Although this sounds like a very simple solution, many language and communication activities still lack diversity in names.

The InterEqual training consists of five self-paced asynchronous online modules designed for autonomous learning, with each of the modules requiring 5–6 hours of work. The activities, referred to as 'Steps' in InterEqual, varied from module to module to engage students in different ways. The methods, among others, included peer learning through action-oriented small group project work and guided online forum discussions; critical (self-)reflective writing; compiling of an individual e-portfolio; and experiential learning – in and outside the classroom – through interaction with a wider university, local, and digital community. In interactions, both inside and outside the group, students practiced active listening and intercultural dialogue skills by engaging in open, empathetic and respectful exchange with people from different backgrounds and of diverse perspectives. These activities helped students understand not only others but themselves as well, raise their cultural self-awareness, analyze their own behavior, and question their approaches to cultural differences.

Box 1 is an example training activity from module 1, followed by excerpts from students' contributions (see Boxes 2 and 3) that demonstrate the diversity of responses. The participants in the online forum were invited to discuss various aspects of their identity that were salient to them in the described context.

Box 1 ONLINE FORUM DISCUSSION ON VALUES AT UNIVERSITY

Source: Module 1 "Increasing Cultural Self-Awareness"

1) **After reflecting on your "Values at University" checklist responses, please consider and answer the following questions:**
    - Where have you identified important cultural differences between your approach and that of people with whom you study together?
    - Are these differences important?

Box 1 (cont.)

- How might these differences become apparent in the studying environment?
- How might others perceive your approach?
- What challenges do these differences present?
- In what ways might you adapt your behavior in order to manage and overcome these cultural differences?

2) **Please respond to at least 2 other participants in the online forum**
Recommended tips for your responses to your classmates:

- Comment on what you found interesting or insightful about their reflections.
- Comment on what their response taught you or made you think differently about.
- Ask clarifying questions that help you to further understand the complexity of their experience.

Box 2 Student 1's contribution to the online forum discussion on values at university

After reflecting on my "Values at University" checklist responses, I've realized a significant cultural difference in my approach compared to that of my peers in the culture I currently study. Primarily, I am less social in getting work done, which has both advantages and challenges in our collaborative environment.

This difference is indeed important. My preference for individual work and focus on tasks without much social interaction contrasts with people who usually prefer to be a bit more social when working together. In the studying or working environment, this difference becomes apparent in group settings. While the people I'm working with engage in discussions and brainstorming sessions, I tend to work independently, processing information internally before presenting it.

People might perceive my approach as aloof or uncooperative. This perception arises from a misunderstanding of my work style, which values deep concentration and minimal distractions. However, it's essential to recognize that this doesn't reflect a lack of interest in teamwork or collaboration. Instead, it's a different method of achieving the same goal.

> Box 2 (cont.)
>
> The primary challenge presented by this difference is the potential for miscommunication and misconceptions. My peers might interpret my quiet, focused demeanor as disinterest or unwillingness to participate, which could hinder collaborative efforts and team cohesion.
>
> To manage and overcome these cultural differences, I'm actively working on adapting my behavior without compromising my core working values. This adaptation involves initiating more frequent communication with my peers, explaining my work process, and actively seeking moments for collaboration. I'm also making an effort to engage more in group discussions, offering my insights while respecting the dynamic nature of team interactions. Additionally, I'm learning to balance between my need for focused work and the team's need for social interaction, finding a middle ground that benefits both my personal productivity and our collective goals.

> Box 3 Student 2's contribution to the online forum discussion on values at university
>
> I have identified cultural differences with the people I study with on campus. Usually, we study together for an exam if we're in the same class or we study together to stay focused and get help from each other on different assignments.
>
> We are from different cultural backgrounds and religions and the differences between us are important.
>
> These differences can be apparent when we decide on a time to meet and study together. For example, another Muslim person in our study group and I prefer to have our studying time when it does not overlap a prayer time. Sometimes, I cannot stay out for too long after dark either since the culture I come from and my parents think it may be dangerous for a woman to be out too late.
>
> People from a similar background/religion as me might be more understanding of where I am coming from since we have similar experiences, unlike people from different backgrounds. A challenge these differences present is having a difficult time scheduling the right time for us to study together. Some of our study group members may have classes that end later in the day or some group members may only have time during prayer times.

> **Box 3 (cont.)**
>
> But we overcome these challenges by communicating. We explain our schedules and responsibilities we have to attend to before scheduling a study session for that week. If a study session overlaps prayer times, we communicate that we need to take a break to pray and my studymates have been very open and accommodating with that. And if we cannot meet on campus due to us only being free at night, we can do our study sessions over video calls on Zoom or Discord.

In addition to completing the module "steps," students were invited to compile an e-portfolio and engage in an action-oriented small group collaborative online project (for details see Golubeva, 2023 and Golubeva, in press).

Recognizing that training needs and interests could vary based on an individual's prior experience, the InterEqual modules were designed in a way that they can be implemented as a stand-alone training session or cohesive training. Students are free to choose which modules to do and complete them in whatever order they want to. Upon completion of the training modules, students are awarded digital badges. And once they complete all five modules, they get a meta-badge (see Figure 9). As of the writing of this Element, 1,150 module-level badges have been conferred, and 221 students were awarded the InterEqual meta-badge for completing the whole program.

4.4 Results of Training Pilot and Students' Feedback

The InterEqual training modules were piloted with more than 200 undergraduate students across different majors representing STEM fields, Humanities, Business, Social Sciences, and Arts. To measure the effectiveness of InterEqual and to evaluate the impact of participation in the training, a mixed-method approach was applied. For quantitative measures, we used pre- and post-training surveys, and pre- and post- results of several self-report assessments (e.g., The Toronto Empathy Questionnaire (TEQ) (Spreng et al., 2009); Interpersonal Reactivity Index (IRI) (Davis, 1980)). For qualitative analysis, data from students' written self-reflections and feedback were collected throughout the training after each of the modules. The input received from students during the pilot was incorporated during the training revisions. Next, I share results collected from the groups where I was the piloting instructor.

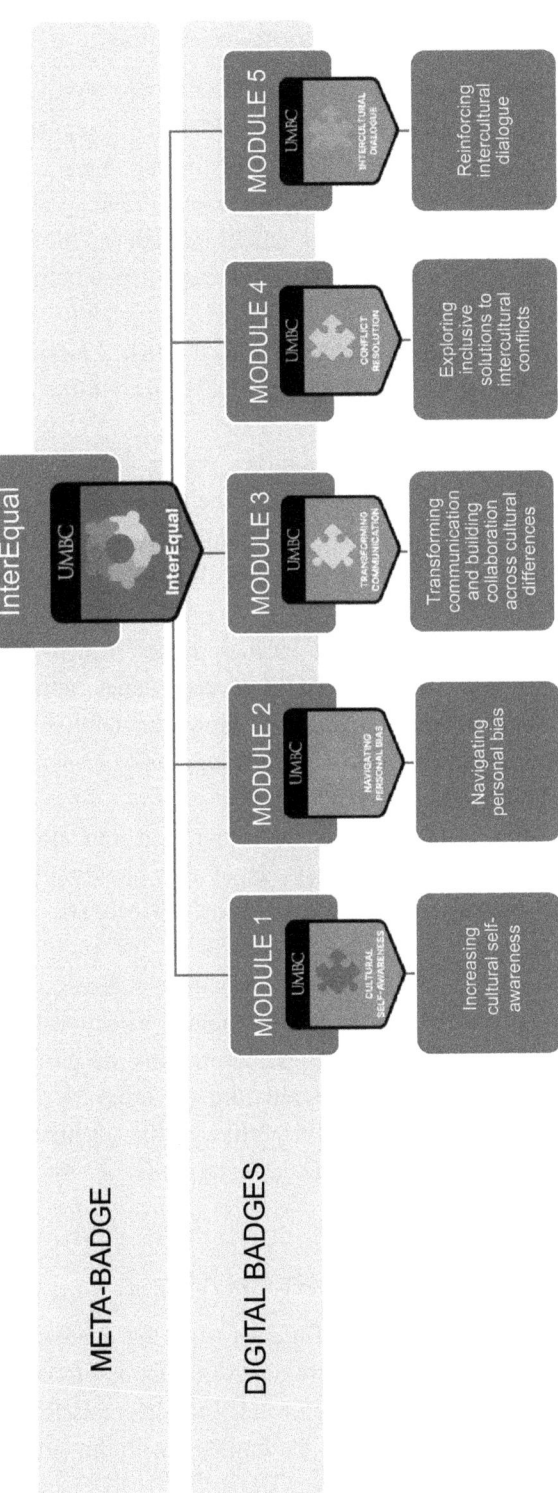

Figure 9 The structure of the InterEqual training (the logos designed by Collin Sullivan and Petra Janka at UMBC in 2022; reproduced with permission)

4.4.1 Results of Quantitative Analysis

The comparative analysis of pre- and post-TEQ scores revealed a notable enhancement in the overall empathy score after the completion of five InterEqual modules. Initially, at the launch of the training pilot, the mean TEQ score stood at 50.70 (SD = 6.59), whereas upon training completion, it rose to 51.86 (SD = 6.76) (n = 162, p = 0.002) (Golubeva, 2023, p. 6). This observed increase of 1.16 is statistically significant (p = 0.002) and can be considered quite valuable.

Regarding perspective-taking, measured with the IRI, a mean increase of 0.41 was observed, from 20.30 (SD = 4.02) to 20.71 (SD = 4.91) (n = 138, p = 0.09) (Golubeva, 2023).

The comparison of the pre- and post-survey results showed a statistically significant increase in students' perception of the campus being diverse and inclusive. Additionally, after the InterEqual training, the number of students who believed that diversity at MSI enhances their experience on campus significantly grew.

When asked to rate their perceived level of importance of 20 RFCDC competences, an increase was observed in several values, attitudes, skills, knowledge and critical understanding areas. However, only in the area of *knowledge and critical understanding of language and communication,* the increase was statistically significant (p = 0.029).

Although we were satisfied with the impact of our training, it is important for us to note some limitations of our quantitative analysis. First, there is no control group in the study, so we are not able to eliminate the possibility that a factor outside of the training modules could explain the changes we found. Additionally, students self-selected into the pilot program, meaning our results include selection bias that we are currently unable to account for. These limitations are part of why we chose a mixed-method design when evaluating the program. The qualitative data highlighted next adds a rich narrative to the quantitative results and increases my confidence in the effectiveness of the InterEqual training.

4.4.2 Results of Qualitative Analysis

In Section 4.4.2, I highlight the main findings from the qualitative analysis following Kirkpatrick's model of training evaluation (Kirkpatrick & Kirkpatrick, 2006), as outlined in Section 4.3.1. I use excerpts from students' self-reflections and feedback to support the findings, with the most important parts of the quotes emphasized in italics.

S22: My main takeaways is *the importance of intercultural communication and the importance of diversity in the workplace and school. I learned that different points of view can provide a lot of value because different cultures may see things differently than you. Diversity in the workplace as well as school can help humans become critical thinkers due to different perspectives.* This idea has helped me *become more open to other perspectives from people who are culturally different from me.*

To summarize, findings from the qualitative analysis correlate with quantitative results, and suggest that the approach taken in the InterEqual training, which combines learning with cooperation on small group telecollaborative projects, was successful in achieving its goals. It is noteworthy to mention that the InterEqual modules are now available for free to all students at the MSI, and will soon be piloted for faculty and staff. Overall, we believe it can serve as an example of how Intercultural Citizenship Education and DEI efforts can be synergized in HE settings.

4.4.3 Reflection on the Process of Piloting the Training Modules

During any pilot of a training program, there may arise numerous potential challenges such as but not limited to participants' recruitment and retention, financial and human resources, infrastructure, and time management. In this section, I will discuss how we managed to avoid or address some of these challenges.

One of the common challenges during the piloting of a training program is ensuring participants' engagement. In the case of InterEqual, we anticipated that participants would exhibit varying levels of commitment and interest. From the outset, we understood the importance of avoiding a "one-size-fits-all" approach to the training program. Our project team invested a significant amount of time (approximately two years) in three critical phases preceding the pilot: (1) needs analysis, (2) training design, and (3) the development of the training modules (see Section 4.3.1). This thorough preparatory process allowed us to design a training program that was specifically tailored to the needs of our current student body, ensuring that the content was both engaging and relevant to them. For example, to enhance students' engagement in online discussions, we built those around their own lived experiences (see, e.g., Boxes 1, 2, and 3). Although this meticulous process was very time-consuming, it significantly contributed to a smoother and less stressful pilot phase, as evidenced by the minimal participant attrition during the pilot semester.

The major challenge we encountered was related to the asynchronous online delivery method. It is important to acknowledge that while the asynchronous format has certain constraints, such as limited real-time interaction, it also offers considerable advantages. For example, this delivery method allowed us to avoid common logistical issues, such as scheduling conflicts and delays, by enabling students to engage with the material at their own pace and on their own schedules. Also, the use of the university's learning management system, to which we had free access, ensured that the pilot did not require additional financial resources. However, the asynchronous nature of the course required intensive communication between students and instructors to maintain engagement and provide timely support. This – in turn – required careful planning and consistent effort to ensure that students felt connected and supported throughout the learning process. To bridge the gap caused by the lack of live interaction, we incorporated small group collaborative projects in our training program, on which students provided very positive feedback (see for students' accounts Section 4.4.2).

Small group project work was essential in achieving the InterEqual learning outcomes (derived from RFCDC) by offering students the opportunity to develop civic-mindedness, self-efficacy, and responsibility, and to practice cooperation skills, empathy, active listening, perspective-taking, communication, and conflict-resolution skills. It is important to mention that it also presented some challenges. Given that in collaborative projects students are highly interdependent, any failure by a group member to complete an assigned task on time can lead to frustration and conflict within the group. We intentionally kept the groups small – 3–5 students; pointed them to digital tools that would facilitate their online collaboration; and also sent reminders, notifying them about upcoming deadlines and alerting them about time-consuming "Steps" (i.e., project tasks) in advance. Under the tough timeline, interpersonal conflicts were unavoidable. However, this had its benefits as students were challenged to develop a self-awareness of their conflict styles and practice skills for resolving the conflicts, meaning they applied the concepts from the course as they were learning them (see for details Golubeva, 2023).

In addition to the aforementioned challenges, the pilot of the training modules required us to continuously monitor and to remain responsive and flexible. We had to make some adjustments in real-time to address emerging issues: for example, to add clarifying guidelines to online activities. This adaptive approach helped to maintain high levels of engagement and had an overall positive effect on participants' satisfaction (see Section 4.4.2).

Overall, while the piloting of the InterEqual training program presented challenges and required a significant joint effort from the colleagues involved in the process, our proactive and strategic approach was instrumental in addressing emerging issues. The lessons learned during the pilot phase were

DEI and Intercultural Citizenship in Higher Education 71

invaluable in refining training activities and preparing the modules for broader implementation.

5 Conclusions and Future Perspectives

5.1 Introduction

In the final section, I summarize the key aspects at the intersections between DEI and Intercultural Citizenship Education, providing recommendations for future research and practice. I also reflect on the challenges and lessons learned from the experience of incorporating DEI training and ICitE into university curricula. I conclude the Element by underscoring that the discussions on DEI and ICitE should continue, urging the Reader to actively engage in intentional efforts in this regard.

5.2 Limitations and Future Research Agenda

The significance of the approach discussed in this Element is that it showed an example of how Intercultural Citizenship Education can be synergized with DEI efforts, considering existing intersections between these two fields. As previously discussed, ICitE and DEI are inherently inter- and transdisciplinary in nature; pursue common goals aimed at raising students' awareness of the importance of human diversity and enhancing the sense of belonging. Both advance the humanistic agenda of HE by emphasizing active civic and social engagement and share the same key attributes (see Figure 2). Given the current absence of a systematic approach to integrating DEI and ICitE in university curricula, a joint effort would be mutually advantageous. The field of Intercultural Citizenship Education – due to its rich theoretical and practical expertise (Alred et al., 2006; Byram, 2008, 2012, 2014, 2021; Byram et al., 2017; Golubeva, 2022; Porto & Yulita, 2017; Ra et al., 2022; Rauschert & Byram, 2018, among many others) – could support DEI initiatives with their well-developed pedagogies; while DEI could provide institutional support for intentional integration of ICitE in higher education. I illustrated through the InterEqual training one example of successful integration of ICitE and DEI on a college campus.

Along with developing values, attitudes, skills, knowledge and critical understanding in areas of RFCDC competence, the InterEqual participants demonstrated an increased sense of belonging to the MSI community and improved perceptions of campus diversity and inclusiveness. The most important outcomes of their intercultural learning and telecollaborative work on small group projects were enhanced empathy and the ability to take the perspectives of others, which play an essential role when communicating with people from diverse backgrounds. Ultimately, this facilitated intercultural dialogue and demonstrated an approach that incorporated a humanistic orientation in HE.

While these results are promising (and dare I say exciting), several limitations to this study should be noted. First, the data collected from students' surveys and self-administered assessments may be subject to social desirability bias. Additionally, as previously discussed, the absence of a control group in the study prevents us from eliminating the possibility that factors external to the training modules may account for the observed changes. Another limitation originates from the sample; specifically, the data were collected solely from a single institution based in the United States and may not be so relevant to universities elsewhere. Nonetheless, it is important to note that our aim was not to develop a "one-size-fits-all" training; instead, we adopted a tailored approach to ensure that the InterEqual program addresses the specific needs of the diverse student community at the MSI.

That being said, while our methodological approach may not be generalizable, it proved to be effective in our context, as supported by the results of quantitative and qualitative analyses. When designing the training, our intention was not to impose it as the "only" or "right" way to synergize DEI and ICitE concepts but rather to demonstrate how such efforts can be undertaken in HE settings while building a training program that met the specific needs of our campus and students.

The main implication of the study findings is that DEI initiatives should adopt a more nuanced and globally informed stance, giving greater attention to linguistic diversity and language and intercultural communication education, as these hold strong potential in fostering competences requisite for an inclusive campus. Intercultural Citizenship Education should address complex themes of power dynamics, privilege, and social justice more comprehensively. It is imperative that research within both ICitE and DEI endeavor to amplify the voices of underrepresented and marginalized communities.

5.3 Final Remarks

Even an optimist will acknowledge that the upcoming decade will pose numerous challenges for humanity in various aspects, including wars and peacebuilding, shortages of drinking water and other resources, digitalization and the use of artificial intelligence, as well as exploration of ocean depths and outer space, and the emergence of new pandemics – just to highlight the most likely ones. These challenges will impact most of us, albeit to varying degrees. Resolving problems related to migration and displacement, access to quality healthcare, climate change, biodiversity loss, and social and economic inequalities will remain global concerns. Effectively addressing these issues necessitates collaborative efforts to build societies that are more sustainable, inclusive, and equitable. We must all mobilize our intercultural citizenship competences.

While current discussions in HE indicate an understanding of the importance of preparing students for intercultural citizenship in a superdiverse world (Baker & Fang, 2022; Barrett & Golubeva, 2022; Byram & Golubeva, 2020; Byram et al., 2017, among others), the current state of the practice does not attest to significant progress (see Golubeva et al., 2018). Similarly, the field of DEI has faced critiques for the ineffectiveness of "well intentioned" but "poorly delivered" policies (Moysiuk, 2019) and for inadequacies in training and pedagogical approaches (see Beeman, 2015). To move forward, both fields need to synergize their efforts, particularly within the context of culturally diverse campuses. This requires the development of curricula that not only recognize diversity but also equip students with the values, attitudes, skills, knowledge and critical understanding necessary for life and work in multicultural, pluralistic societies.

I do not deny that achieving this goal is complicated by the contentious and divisive political rhetoric surrounding DEI. Thus, in linking ICitE with DEI, I emphasize their potential to jointly prepare students for active engagement in diverse social contexts. While doing this, practitioners of both fields cannot ignore or be naive to the political debates associated with DEI (and to a lesser extent ICitE) and must thoughtfully identify what a more synergized approach could look like in their given political and institutional context.

In the practical example presented in this Element, I have summarized the key points of intersection between DEI and ICitE, provided recommendations for research and practice moving forward, and reflected on the challenges and lessons learned from the experience of incorporating DEI training and Intercultural Citizenship Education into university curricula. It is important for Readers to recognize that there are no universal solutions and ready recipes in the field of education, particularly when we want our students to have agency and serve as the experts of their own experiences, needs, and understanding of the world. The InterEqual framework, developed by me and my colleagues, is just an example that in our context worked well and had a positive impact on students and their sense of belonging. However, in the case of Readers' institutions, other content and methods may be required and should be considered. Nevertheless, I hope that the insights shared in this Element will prove useful.

I encourage Readers to actively make intentional efforts in this direction: create their own frameworks for integrating DEI and ICitE in their own work, apply them in practical settings, and share their insights and learning with the broader field. I firmly believe that synergizing Diversity, Equity, and Inclusion and Intercultural Citizenship Education opens new opportunities for advancing the humanistic agenda in HE. However, due to the inherent complexities and challenges involved, further theoretical and pedagogical inquiries are essential. I look forward to learning from how other scholars and practitioners intentionally approach the integration of DEI and ICitE into their own work and communities.

Funding

This work was supported by the UMBC Center for Social Science Scholarship Summer Fellowship.

References

ABC News Australia. (2022, April 17). *Desperate scenes in Shanghai amid harsh lockdown.* [Video] www.youtube.com/watch?v=Xg9A7mWo8l8.

Abcarian, R. (2024, January 7). *Opinion: The resignation of Harvard's Claudine Gay is touted as a DEI failure, but that's hardly the case.* Los Angeles Times. Accessed February 10, 2024, from www.latimes.com/opinion/story/2024-01-07/harvard-claudine-gay-christopher-rufo-diversity-equity-inclusion.

Adams, C., & Chiwaya, N. (2024, March 2). *Map: See which states have introduced or passed anti-DEI bills.* NBC News. Accessed on March 15, 2024, from www.nbcnews.com/data-graphics/anti-dei-bills-states-republican-lawmakers-map-rcna140756.

Adams, M., Blumenfeld, W. J., Castañeda, C., et al. (Eds.) (2013). *Readings for Diversity and Social Justice. 3rd Edition.* New York: Routledge.

Agar, M. (1994). *Language Shock: Understanding the Culture of Conversation.* New York: William Morrow.

Aktas, F., Pitts, K., Richards, J. C., & Silova, I. (2017). Institutionalizing global citizenship: A critical analysis of higher education programs and curricula. *Journal of Studies in International Education, 21,* 65–80.

Alred, A., Byram, M., & Fleming, M. (Eds.) (2006). *Education for Intercultural Citizenship. Concepts and Comparisons.* Clevedon: Multilingual Matters.

Anderson, L. W., & Krathwohl, D. R. (2001). *A Taxonomy for Learning, Teaching, and Assessing: A Revision of Bloom's Taxonomy of Educational Objectives. Complete Edition.* New York: Longman.

Andreotti, V. (2011). *Actionable Postcolonial Theory in Education.* New York: Palgrave Macmillan.

Annie E. Casey Foundation (2014). *Race Equity and Inclusion Action Guide.* Baltimore, MD: Annie E. Casey Foundation.

Aykol, E., Kapetanakos, D., & Lehman, R. (2021). From campus to the world: Global learning in the context of an urban community college. *New Directions for Community Colleges, 2021*(195), 37–51.

Baker, B. (2024). The challenge of implementing DEI policies – a case study. (July 15, 2024). SSRN: https://ssrn.com/abstract=4898680 or http://dx.doi.org/10.2139/ssrn.4898680.

Baker, W., Boonsuk, Y., Ra, J. J., Sangiamchit, C., & Snodin, N. (2022). Thai study abroad students as intercultural citizens: Developing intercultural citizenship through English medium education and ELT. *Asia Pacific Journal of Education*, 1–16. https://doi.org/10.1080/02188791.2022.2096569.

Baker, W., & Fang, F. (2021). "So maybe I'm a global citizen": Developing intercultural citizenship in English medium education. *Language, Culture and Curriculum, 34*(1), 1–17. https://doi.org/10.1080/07908318.2020.1748045.

Baker, W., & Fang, F. (2022). Intercultural citizenship and the internationalisation of higher education: The role of English language teaching. *Journal of English as a Lingua Franca, 11*(1), 63–75.

Barger, A. (2023, April 28). *Is there a diversity issue among chief diversity officers?* Fastcompany.com. Accessed on March 1, 2024, from www.fastcompany.com/90888117/is-there-a-diversity-issue-among-chief-diversity-officers.

Barnett, R. (1997). *Higher Education: A Critical Business.* Buckingham: Open University Press.

Barnett, R. (2000). *Realising the University in an Age of Supercomplexity.* Buckingham: Open University Press.

Barnett, R. (2011). The coming of the ecological university. *Oxford Review of Education, 37*(4), 439–455. https://doi.org/10.1080/03054985.2011.595550.

Barnett, R. (2023). Only connect: Designing university futures. *Quality in Higher Education, 29*(1), 116–131. https://doi.org/10.1080/13538322.2022.2100627.

Barrett, M. (2016). *Competences for Democratic Culture: Living Together as Equals in Culturally Diverse Democratic Societies.* Strasbourg: Council of Europe.

Barrett, M., & Byram, M. (2022). *Autobiography of Intercultural Encounters: Context, Concepts and Theories.* Strasbourg: Council of Europe.

Barrett, M., Byram, M., Lázár, I., Mompoint-Gaillard, P., & Philippou, S. (2014). *Developing Intercultural Competence through Education.* Strasbourg: Council of Europe.

Barrett, M., & Golubeva, I. (2022). From intercultural communicative competence to intercultural citizenship: Preparing young people for citizenship in a culturally diverse democratic world. In T. McConachy, I. Golubeva, & M. Wagner (Eds.), *Intercultural Learning in Language Education and Beyond: Evolving Concepts, Perspectives and Practices* (pp. 60–83). Bristol: Multilingual Matters.

Beeman, A. (2015). Teaching to convince, teaching to empower: Reflections on student resistance and self-defeat at predominantly white vs. racially diverse campuses. *The Journal for Understanding and Dismantling Privilege, 5*(1), 13–33.

Bennett, M. J. (1993). Towards ethnorelativism: A developmental model of intercultural sensitivity. In R. M. Paige (Ed.), *Education for the Intercultural Experience* (pp. 21–71). Yarmouth, ME: Intercultural Press.

Bhabha, H. K. (2006). Culture's in between. In S. Hall, & P. Du Gay (Eds.), *Questions of Cultural Identity* (pp. 53–60). London: Sage.

Bhasin, D. (2022). *"DEI fatigue": It's time for some home truths*. Flexability. Accessed on March 15, 2024, from www.flexability.com/opinion/2022/dei-fatigue-its-time-for-some-home-truths.

Bloom, B. S. (Ed.) (1956). *Taxonomy of Educational Objectives: The Classification of Educational Goals. Handbook I.* London: Longman.

Blum, N., Berlin, A., Isaacs, A., Burch, W. J., & Willott, C. (2019). Medical students as global citizens: A qualitative study of medical students' views on global health teaching within the undergraduate medical curriculum. *BMC Medical Education, 19*, 1–9.

Boonsuk, Y., & Fang, F. (2023). Re-envisaging English medium instruction, intercultural citizenship development, and higher education in the context of studying abroad. *Language and Education, 37*(3), 271–287. https://doi.org/10.1080/09500782.2021.1996595.

Bowleg, L. (2008). When black + lesbian + woman ≠ black lesbian woman: The methodological challenges of qualitative and quantitative intersectionality research. *Sex Roles, 59*(5–6), 312–325.

Box, G. E. P., Luceño, A., & Paniagua-Quiñones, M. del Carmen (2009). *Statistical Control by Monitoring and Adjustment. 2nd Edition.* Hoboken, NJ: John Wiley & Sons.

Branson, R. K. (1978). The interservice procedures for instructional systems development. *Educational Technology, 18*(3), 11–14.

Branson, R. K., Rayner, G. T., Cox, J. L., et al. (1975). *Interservice Procedures for Instructional Systems Development: Executive Summary and Model.* Tallahassee, FL: Center for Educational Technology, Florida State University.

British Council. (2013). *Culture at work: The value of intercultural skills in the workplace.* Accessed on November 20, 2023, from www.britishcouncil.org/sites/default/files/culture-at-work-report-v2.pdf.

Buckingham, D. (2008). *Introducing Identity.* Chicago, IL: MacArthur Foundation Digital Media and Learning Initiative.

Byram, M. (1997). *Teaching and Assessing Intercultural Communicative Competence.* Clevedon: Multilingual Matters.

Byram, M. (2008). *From Foreign Language Education to Education for Intercultural Citizenship: Essays and Reflections.* Clevedon: Multilingual Matters.

Byram, M. (2012). Conceptualizing intercultural (communicative) competence and intercultural citizenship. In J. Jackson (Ed.) *Routledge Handbook of Language and Intercultural Communication* (pp. 85–97). New York: Routledge.

Byram, M. (2014). Twenty-five years on – from cultural studies to intercultural citizenship. *Language, Culture and Curriculum, 27*(3), 209–225. https://doi.org/10.1080/07908318.2014.974329.

Byram, M. (2018). An essay on internationalism in foreign language education. *Intercultural Communication Education, 1*(2), 64–82. https://doi.org/10.29140/ice.v1n2.54.

Byram, M. (2021). *Teaching and Assessing Intercultural Communicative Competence: Revisited*. Bristol: Multilingual Matters.

Byram, M., Barrett, M., Aroni, A., et al. (2021). *A Portfolio of Competences for Democratic Culture: Standard Version*. Strasbourg: Council of Europe. Accessed June 10, 2023, from https://rm.coe.int/0900001680a256af.

Byram, M., Barrett, M., Ipgrave, J., Jackson, R., & Méndez García, M. C. (2009a). *Autobiography of Intercultural Encounters*. Strasbourg: Council of Europe. Accessed March 11, 2024, from www.coe.int/en/web/autobiography-intercultural-encounters/autobiography-of-intercultural-encounters.

Byram, M., Barrett, M., Ipgrave, J., Jackson, R., & Méndez García, M. C. (2009b). *Autobiography of Intercultural Encounters: Notes for Facilitators*. Strasbourg: Council of Europe. Accessed March 11, 2024, from www.coe.int/en/web/autobiography-intercultural-encounters/autobiography-of-intercultural-encounters.

Byram, M., & Golubeva, I. (2020). Conceptualizing intercultural (communicative) competence and intercultural citizenship. In J. Jackson (Ed.) *Routledge Handbook of Language and Intercultural Communication, 2nd Edition* (pp. 70–85). London: Routledge.

Byram, M., Golubeva, I., Han, H., & Wagner, M. (Eds.) (2017). *From Principles to Practice in Education for Intercultural Citizenship*. Bristol: Multilingual Matters.

Byram, M., Golubeva, I., & Porto, M. (2022). Internationalism, democracy, political education – an agenda for foreign language education. In C. Lütge, T. Merse, & P. Rauschert (Eds.), *Global Citizenship in Foreign Language Education: Concepts, Practices, Connections* (pp. 128–150). New York: Routledge.

Carlton, G. (2023). *Professor gender pay gap: Colleges haven't fixed it. Will courts?* Best Colleges. Accessed on March 11, 2024, from www.bestcolleges.com/news/analysis/professor-gender-pay-gap-colleges-havent-fixed-it-will-courts/#:~:

text=The%20Gender%20Pay%20Gap%20in,of%20University%20Professors%20(AAUP).

Carothers, T. (2020, October 15). *The global rise of anti-lockdown protests – and what to do about it*. World Politics Review. Accessed on January 8, 2024, from www.worldpoliticsreview.com/amid-the-covid-19-pandemic-protest-movements-challenge-lockdowns-worldwide/.

CBS/News Service of Florida. (2023, May 15). *DeSantis curtails diversity, equity & inclusion programs at state colleges*. CBS News. Accessed on March 15, 2024, from www.cbsnews.com/miami/news/desantis-signs-bill-targeting-diversity-inclusion-program-at-florida-colleges/.

Center for American Women in Politics. (2023). *Women Serving in the 118th Congress (2023–2025)*. Rutgers – New Brunswick: Eagleton Institute of Politics. Accessed on December 1, 2023, from https://cawp.rutgers.edu/facts/levels-office/congress/women-serving-118th-congress-2023-2025.

Chen, C. W., & Gorski, P. C. (2015). Burnout in social justice and human rights activists: Symptoms, causes, and implications. *Journal of Human Rights Practice*, 7(3): 366–390. https://doi.org/10.1093/jhuman/huv011.

Cho, S., Crenshaw, K. W., & McCall, L. (2013). Toward a field of intersectionality studies: Theory, applications, and praxis. *Signs: Journal of Women in Culture and Society*, 38(4), 785–810.

Cloud, D. (2018). *From austerity to attacks on scholars*. Inside Higher Ed. Accessed on March 8, 2024, from www.insidehighered.com/views/2018/05/03/neoliberal-academy-age-trump.

Council of Europe (CoE). (2008). *White Paper on Intercultural Dialogue*. Strasbourg: Council of Europe.

Council of Europe (CoE). (2016). *Competences for Democratic Culture: Living Together as Equals in Culturally Diverse Democratic Societies*. Strasbourg: Council of Europe. Accessed on April 12, 2021, from https://rm.coe.int/16806ccc07.

Council of Europe (CoE). (2018). *Reference Framework of Competences for Democratic Culture* [3 volumes]. Accessed on April 12, 2021, from www.coe.int/en/web/reference-framework-of-competences-for-democratic-culture/rfcdc-volumes.

Crenshaw, K. W. (1989). Demarginalizing the intersection of race and sex: A black feminist critique of antidiscrimination doctrine, feminist theory and antiracist politics. *The University of Chicago Legal Forum*, 1989(1), 139–167.

Crenshaw, K. W. (1991). Mapping the margins: Intersectionality, identity politics, and violence against women of color. *Stanford Law Review*, 43(6), 1241–1299.

Crutchfield, R., & Maguire, J. (2018). *Study of student basic needs*. California State University Basic Needs Initiative. Accessed on March 8, 2024, from www.calstate.edu/impact-of-the-csu/student-success/basic-needs-initiative/Documents/phaseII-report-with-Appendix.pdf.

Dan Hirleman, E. (2011). Education of global engineers and global citizens. In G. L. Downey, & K. Beddoes (Eds.), *What Is Global Engineering Education For? The Making of International Educators, Part I & II. Synthesis Lectures on Global Engineering* (pp. 93–108). Cham: Springer. https://doi.org/10.1007/978-3-031-02124-4_4.

Davis, M. H. (1980). A multidimensional approach to individual differences in empathy. *JSAS Catalog of Selected Documents in Psychology, 10*, 85.

Davis, M. H. (1983). Measuring individual differences in empathy: Evidence for a multidimensional approach. *Journal of Personality and Social Psychology, 44*, 113–126. https://doi.org/10.1037/0022-3514.44.1.113.

Day, H. R. (1983). Race relations training in the military. In D. Landis, & R. Brislin (Eds.), *Handbook of Intercultural Training, Vol. II: Issues in Training Methodology* (pp. 241–289). New York: Pergamon Press.

Deardorff, D. K. (2006). The identification and assessment of intercultural competence. *Journal of Studies in International Education, 10*(3), 241–266. https://doi.org/10.1177/1028315306287002.

Desilver, D. (2022, March 10). *The polarization in today's Congress has roots that go back decades*. Pew Research Center. Accessed March 17, 2024, from www.pewresearch.org/short-reads/2022/03/10/the-polarization-in-todays-congress-has-roots-that-go-back-decades/.

Dessel, A., Rogge, M. E., & Garlington, S. B. (2006). Using intergroup dialogue to promote social justice and change. *Social Work, 51*(4), 303–315.

Devine, P. G., & Monteith, M. J. (1993). The role of discrepancy associated affect in prejudice reduction. In D. Mackie, & D. Hamilton (Eds.) *Affect, Cognition, and Stereotyping: Interactive Processes in Group Perception* (pp.137–166). San Diego, CA: Harcourt, Brace, & Jananovich.

De Wit, H. (2010). Global citizenship and study abroad: A European comparative perspective. In R. Lewin (Ed.), *The Handbook of Practice and Research in Study Abroad: Higher Education and the Quest for Global Citizenship* (pp. 234–251). New York: Routledge.

DiAngelo, R. (2022). *White Fragility: Why Understanding Racism Can Be So Hard for White People (Adapted for Young Adults)*. Boston, MA: Beacon Press.

Dooly, M. (2006). Integrating intercultural competence and citizenship education into teacher training: A pilot project. *Citizenship Teaching and Learning, 2*(1), 18–30.

Dover, T. L., Major, B., & Kaiser, C. R. (2014). Diversity initiatives, status, and system-justifying beliefs: When and how diversity efforts de-legitimize discrimination claims. *Group Processes & Intergroup Relations*, *17*(4), 485–493.

Dower, N. (2008). Are we all global citizens, or are only some of us global citizens? The relevance of this question to education. In A. Abdi, & L. Shultz (Eds.), *Educating for Human Rights and Global Citizenship* (pp. 39–53). Albany, NY: SUNY Press.

Duignan, B. (2024). Social justice. In *Encyclopaedia Britannica*. Accessed on September 18, 2024 from www.britannica.com/topic/social-justice.

Elvin, H. L. (1960). Nationalism and internationalism in education. *The School Review*, *68*(1) 1–22.

Equality Act. (2010). *Equality Act*. The Stationary Office, London. Accessed on Mar 1, 2024 from www.legislation.gov.uk/ukpga/2010/15/pdfs/ukpga_20100015_en.pdf.

Equality and Human Rights Commission (2018). *Understanding equality*. Accessed on May 5, 2020 from www.equalityhumanrights.com/en/contact-us.

European Commission (EC) (2018a). *Erasmus+ Programme Guide. Version 3 (2018): 10/08/2018*. Accessed January 8, 2024, from https://erasmus-plus.ec.europa.eu/sites/default/files/erasmus-plus-programme-guide3_en.pdf.

European Commission (EC). (2018b). *Report on Equality between Men and Women in the EU*. Luxembourg: Publications Office of the European Union.

European Commission (EC). (2019). *Erasmus+ Higher Education Impact Study*. Accessed April 12, 2021, from https://op.europa.eu/en/publication-detail/-/publication/94d97f5c-7ae2-11e9-9f05-01aa75ed71a1/language-en.

European Parliament (EP). (2015). *Report on the role of intercultural dialogue, cultural diversity and education in promoting EU fundamental values*. December 21, 2015 – (2015/2139(INI)). Accessed May 10, 2023, from www.europarl.europa.eu/doceo/document/A-8-2015-0373_EN.html.

Eurostat. (2022). *Gender pay gap in unadjusted form*. Accessed on March 15, 2024, from https://ec.europa.eu/eurostat.

Fang, F., & Baker, W. (2018). "A more inclusive mind towards the world": English language teaching and study abroad in China from intercultural citizenship and English as a lingua franca perspectives. *Language Teaching Research*, *22*(5), 608–624.

Fantini, A. (2009). Assessing intercultural competence: Issues and tools. In D. K. Deardorff (Ed.), *The SAGE Handbook of Intercultural Competence* (pp. 456–476). Thousand Oaks, CA: Sage.

Fenn, J., & Irvin, C. G. (2005). *Do You See What I See?: A Diversity Tale for Retaining People of Color*. San Francisco, CA: Pfeiffer.

Gibbs, G. (1988). *Learning by Doing: A Guide to Teaching and Learning Methods*. Oxford, UK: Further Education Unit at Oxford Politechnic.

Glanzman, A. (2024, January 2). *Gay resigned as Harvard's president on Tuesday after a new round of plagiarism accusations*. The New York Times. Accessed on January 3, 2024, from www.nytimes.com/2024/01/02/us/claudine-gay-resignation-letter-harvard.html.

Goldmann, K. (1994). *The Logic of Internationalism: Coercion and Accommodation*. London: Routledge.

Goldrick-Rab, S., Baker-Smith, C., Coca, V., Looker, E., & Williams, T. (2019). *College and-university basic needs insecurity: A national #RealCollege survey report: The hope-center for college, community, and justice*. Temple University: Philadelphia, PA. Accessed on January 3, 2024, from https://tacc.org/sites/default/files/documents/2019-04/hope_realcollege_report.pdf.

Golubeva, I. (2020). Enhancing faculty and staff engagement in internationalisation: A Hungarian example of training through intercultural dialogue. In U. Lundgren, P. Castro, & J. Woodin (Eds.), *Educational Approaches to Internationalisation through Intercultural Dialogue: Reflections on Theory and Practice* (pp. 183–194). New York: Routledge.

Golubeva, I. (2022). Intercultural citizenship education in university settings. In R. Desjardins, & S. Wiksten (Eds.), *Handbook of Civic Engagement and Education* (pp. 191–209). Northampton, MA: Edward Elgar.

Golubeva, I. (2023). Raising students' self-awareness of their conflict communication styles: Insights from an intercultural telecollaboration project. *Societies*, *13*(10), 223. https://doi.org/10.3390/soc13100223.

Golubeva, I. (in press). Digital humanities pedagogy in action: Insights from intercultural telecollaboration exploring inclusiveness of university campuses through art. *Language and Intercultural Communication*.

Golubeva, I., Di Maria, D., Holden, A., Kohler, K., & Wade, M. E. (forthcoming). Exploring students' perceptions of the campus climate and intergroup relations: Insights from a campus-wide survey at a minority serving university.

Golubeva, I., Gómez Parra, Mª E., & Espejo Mohedano, R. (2018). What does "active citizenship" mean for Erasmus students? *Intercultural Education*, *29*(1), 40–58.

Golubeva, I., & Guntersdorfer, I. (2020). Addressing empathy in intercultural virtual exchange: A preliminary framework. In M. Hauck, & A. Müller-Hartmann (Eds.), *Virtual Exchange and 21st Century Teacher Education: Short Papers from the 2019 EVALUATE Conference* (pp. 117–126).

Accessed on May 1, 2021, from https://research-publishing.net/manuscript?10.14705/rpnet.2020.46.1137.

Golubeva, I., & Porto, M. (2022). Educating democratically and interculturally competent citizens: A virtual exchange between university students in Argentina and the USA. *Iranian Journal of Language Teaching Research*, *10*(3), 9–27. https://doi.org/10.30466/ijltr.2022.121223.

Golubeva, I., Wagner, M., & Yakimowski, M. E. (2017). Comparing students' perceptions of global citizenship in Hungary and the USA. In M. Byram, I. Golubeva, H. Han, & M. Wagner (Eds.), *From Principles to Practice in Education for Intercultural Citizenship* (pp. 3–24). Bristol: Multilingual Matters.

Grenny, J., Patterson, K., McMillan, R., Switzler, A., & Gregory, E. (2022). *Crucial Conversations. 3rd Edition*. New York: McGraw Hill.

Griffin, S. R. (2021, February 6). *Where "Diversity Training" Goes Wrong*. Medium. Accessed on March 25, 2024, from https://medium.com/@shaylargriffin/where-diversity-training-goes-wrong-10-essential-questions-to-ask-1217863eab04.

Guardian News. (2022, April 11). *Residents in locked down Shanghai scream from their balconies: "This cannot last"* [Video]. YouTube. www.youtube.com/watch?v=RBJj_UwkSyc.

Guarino, C. M., & Borden, V. M. (2017). Faculty service loads and gender: Are women taking care of the academic family? *Research in Higher Education*, *58*, 672–694. https://doi.org/10.1007/s11162-017-9454-2.

Gudykunst, W. B. (1993). Toward effective interpersonal and intergroup communication. In R. J. Wiseman, & J. Koester (Eds.), *Intercultural Communication Competence (International and Intercultural Communication Annual*, Volume 16. pp. 3–71). Thousand Oaks, CA: Sage.

Guntersdorfer, I., & Golubeva, I. (2018). Emotional intelligence and intercultural competence: Theoretical questions and pedagogical possibilities. *Intercultural Communication Education*, *1*(2), 54–63. https://doi.org/10.29140/ice.v1n2.60.

Gurin, P., Nagda, B. A., & Sorensen, N. (2011). Intergroup dialogue: Education for a broad conception of civic engagement. *Liberal Education*, *97*(2), 46–51.

Hall, E. T. (1976). *Beyond Culture*. New York: Doubleday.

Hall, S., & Du Gay, P. (Eds.) (2006). *Questions of Cultural Identity*. London: Sage.

Halliday, F. (1988). Three concepts of internationalism. *International Affairs*, *64*, 187–198.

Han, H., Song, L., Jing, H., & Zhao, Y. (2017). Exploring perceptions of intercultural citizenship among English learners in Chinese universities. In

M. Byram, I. Golubeva, H. Han, & M. Wagner (eds.), *From Principles to Practice in Education for Intercultural Citizenship* (pp. 25–44). Bristol: Multilingual Matters.

Hanley, R. (2023). Defense against the dark arts: Academic freedom meets the antiwoke crusade. Accessed on August 20, 2024, from www.aaup.org/sites/default/files/Hanley_JAF14.pdf.

Hanlon, A. R. (2023, October 23). *West Virginia University Is Everything That's Wrong with Higher Education Today*. New Republic. Accessed on December 14, 2023, from https://newrepublic.com/article/176202/west-virginia-university-higher-education-enrollment-cliff-cuts.

Harper, S. R., & Hurtado, S. (2007). Nine themes in campus racial climates and implications for institutional transformation. In Harper, S. R. & Patton, L. D. (Eds.), *Responding to the Realities of Race on Campus. New Directions for Student Services* (No. 120, pp. 7–24). San Francisco, CA: Jossey-Bass. https://doi.org/10.1002/ss.254.

Hart, J., & Fellabaum, J. (2008). Analyzing campus climate studies: Seeking to define and understand. *Journal of Diversity in Higher Education*, *1*(4), 222–234. https://doi.org/10.1037/a0013627.

Heidegger, M. (1962). *Being and Time*. Oxford: Blackwell.

Helms, J. E. (1995). An update of Helms's White and people of color racial identity models. In J. G. Ponterotto, J. M. Casas, L. A. Suzuki, & C. M. Alexander (Eds.), *Handbook of Multicultural Counseling* (pp. 181–198). Thousand Oaks, CA: Sage.

Herbert, J. M. (2023). Academic free speech or right-wing grievance? *Digital Discovery*, *2*, 260–297. https://doi.org/10.1039/D2DD00111J.

Hmielowski, J. D., Hutchens, M. J., & Beam, M. A. (2020). Asymmetry of Partisan media effects?: Examining the reinforcing process of conservative and liberal media with political beliefs. *Political Communication*, *37*(6), 852–868. https://doi.org/10.1080/10584609.2020.1763525.

Hoffart, A. R. (2023). *Interpreting Intersectionality: Interpretative Politics in Metacommentaries*. London: Routledge.

Hoffman, M., Richmond, J., Morrow, J., & Salomone, K. (2003). Investigating "sense of belonging" in first-year college students. *Journal of College Student Retention*, *4*(3), 227–256.

Holliday, A. R. (2011). *Intercultural Communication and Ideology*. London: Sage.

Hsu, A. (2023, August 19). *Corporate DEI initiatives are facing cutbacks and legal attacks*. National Public Radio. Accessed on March 15, 2024, from www.npr.org/2023/08/19/1194595310/dei-affirmative-action-supreme-court-layoffs-diversity-equity-inclusion.

Humphreys, G. (2023). Short-term student exchanges and intercultural learning. *Elements in Intercultural Communication*. Cambridge: Cambridge University Press.

Hunt, K. P. (2016). From paper to plastic: Electronic benefits transfer as technology of-neoliberalization. *Communication and Critical/Cultural Studies, 13*(4), 380–399. https://doi.org/10.1080/14791420.2016.1194521.

Hunt, V., Prince, S., Dixon-Fyle, S., & Yee, L. (2018). Delivering through diversity: Execute Summary. *McKinsey & Company, 231*, 1–39.

Hurtado, S., Alvarez, C. L., Guillermo-Wann, C., Cuellar, M., & Arellano, L. (2012). A model for diverse learning environments: The scholarship on creating and assessing conditions for student success. *Higher Education: Handbook of Theory and Research, 27*, 41–122.

Hurtado, S., & Ruiz Alvarado, A. (2012). *The Climate for Underrepresented Groups and Diversity on Campus*. Los Angeles, CA: Higher Education Research Institute.

Ingram, D. C. (2012). College students' sense of belonging: Dimensions and correlates. Doctoral Dissertation. Stanford, CA: Stanford University. https://purl.stanford.edu/rd771tq2209.

Jeanne Clery Disclosure of Campus Security Policy and Campus Crime Statistics Act of 1990, 20 U.S.C. §1092(f) (2018).

Jenkins, J. (2006). Current perspectives on teaching world Englishes and English as a lingua franca. *TESOL Quarterly, 40*(1), 157–181. https://doi.org/10.2307/40264515.

Jimenez, C. (2019). *New Survey of California Community College Students Reveals More than-Half Face Food Insecurity and Nearly 20 Percent Have Faced Homelessness*. California Community Colleges. Accessed on January 3, 2024, from www.cccco.edu/About-Us/News-and-Media/Press-Releases/Food-Insecurity-Homelessness.

Jiménez-Castillo, G., Partal-Ureña, A. J., Fernández-Carrasco, J. I., Muñoz-Rodríguez, F. J., & Hontoria, L. (2021). Education for sustainable development: Take action, what can we do? *INTED2021 Proceedings, 6372–6376*. https://doi.org/10.21125/inted.2021.1273.

Johnson, P. R., Boyer, M. A., & Brown, S. W. (2011). Vital interests: Cultivating global competence in the international studies classroom. *Globalisation, Societies and Education, 9*, 503–519. http://dx.doi.org/10.1080/14767724.2011.605331.

Kachru, B. B. (1997). World Englishes and English-using communities. *Annual Review of Applied Linguistics, 17*, 66–87. https://doi.org/10.1017/S0267190500003287World.

Kaiser, C. R., Major, B., Jurcevic, I., et al. (2013). Presumed fair: Ironic effects of organizational diversity structures. *Journal of Personality and Social Psychology*, *104*, 504–519. https://doi.org/10.1037/a0030838.

Kennedy, D. (2022, February 5). *Photo shows UK PM Boris Johnson partying during 2020 COVID lockdown*. New York Post. Accessed on January 8, 2024, from https://nypost.com/2022/02/05/photo-shows-boris-johnson-with-beer-at-2020-birthday-party/.

Kingson, J. A. (2023, September 3). *West Virginia's foreign language cuts could be a "blueprint" for higher ed attacks*. Axios. Accessed on September 30, 2023, from www.axios.com/2023/08/30/west-virginia-university-foreign-language-classes.

Kirkpatrick, D. L., & Kirkpatrick, J. (2006). *Evaluating Training Programs: The Four Levels. 3rd Edition*. San Francisco, CA: Berrett-Koehler.

Kishino, H., & Takahashi, T. (2019). Global citizenship development: Effects of study abroad and other factors. *Journal of International Students*, *9*(2), 535–559.

Kolb, D. A. (1984). *Experiential Learning: Experience as the Source of Learning and Development*. Englewood Cliffs, NJ: Prentice Hall.

Kramsch, C. (1993). *Context and Culture in Language Teaching*. Oxford: Oxford University Press.

Kramsch, C. (2020). *Language as Symbolic Power*. Cambridge: Cambridge University Press.

Labaree, L. W. (Ed.) (1959). *The Papers of Benjamin Franklin*, Vol. 1, January 6, 1706 through December 31, 1734 (pp. 27–30). New Haven, CT: Yale University Press.

Laing, S. (2022, September 21). *Do you have "diversity fatigue"? People doing DEI work often face frustration, isolation*. The Globe and Mail. Accessed on March 15, 2024, from www.theglobeandmail.com/business/article-do-you-have-diversity-fatigue-people-doing-dei-work-often-face/.

Lantz-Deaton, C., & Golubeva, I. (2020). *Intercultural Competence for College and University Students: A Global Guide for Employability and Social Change*. Cham: Springer.

Linder, C. (2016). Working with white college students to understand and navigate white racial identities. In M. J. Cuyjet, C. Linder, M. F. Howard-Hamilton, & D. L. Cooper (Eds.), *Multiculturalism on Campus* (pp. 208–231). New York: Routledge.

Lipman, J. (2018, January 25). *Diversity training fails American companies*. Time. Accessed on February 12, 2024, from https://time.com/5118035/diversitytraining-infuriates-men-fails-women/.

Lundgren, U., Castro, P., & Woodin, J. (Eds.) (2020). *Educational Approaches to Internationalisation through Intercultural Dialogue: Reflections on Theory and Practice*. New York: Routledge.

Lustig, M. W., & Koester, J. (2010). *Intercultural Competence: Interpersonal Communication across Cultures*. London: Pearson.

May, V. M. (2015). *Pursuing Intersectionality, Unsettling Dominant Imaginaries*. New York: Routledge.

McConachy, T., Golubeva, I., & Wagner, M. (Eds.) (2022). *Intercultural Learning in Language Education and Beyond: Evolving Concepts, Perspectives and Practices*. Bristol: Multilingual Matters.

McKenzie, S. (2019, May 16). *Sex vouchers for migrants? The truth behind Europe's fake stories*. CNN. Accessed on December 10, 2023, from www.cnn.com/2019/05/16/europe/populism-fake-news-european-elections-intl/index.html.

Menand, L. (2020, January 13). *The changing meaning of affirmative action*. The New Yorker. Accessed on March 27, 2023, from www.newyorker.com/magazine/2020/01/20/have-we-outgrown-the-need-for-affirmative-action.

Mitchell, K. (2012). Student mobility and European identity: Erasmus study as a civic experience? *Journal of Contemporary European Research*, *8*(4), 490–518.

Moysiuk, J. (2019). A critique of diversity, inclusion and equity policies in Canadian universities. *Political Science Undergraduate Review*, *4*(1), 65–71.

Myers, J. P. (2006). Rethinking the social studies curriculum in the context of globalization: Education for global citizenship in the US. *Theory & Research in Social Education*, *34*, 370–394. http://dx.doi.org/10.1080/00933104.2006.10473313.

Nash, J. C. (2017). Intersectionality and its discontents. *American Quarterly*, *69*(1), 117–129.

National Center for Education Statistics (NCES). (2017). *Bachelor's, master's, and doctor's degrees conferred by postsecondary institutions, by sex of student and discipline division: 2015–16*. NCES. Accessed on March 15, 2024, from https://nces.ed.gov/programs/digest/d17/tables/dt17_318.30.asp?current=yes.

National Institutes of Health (NIH). (2017). NIH Glossary [Internet]. Accessed on August 1, 2018 from (https://diversity.nih.gov/find-read-learn/glossary).

Nussbaum, M. C. (1999). *Sex and Social Justice*. Oxford: Oxford University Press.

Nussbaum, M. C. (2002). Education for citizenship in an era of global connection. *Studies in Philosophy and Education*, *21*, 289–303. https://doi.org/10.1023/A:1019837105053.

Nussbaum, M. C. (2006). Education and democratic citizenship: Capabilities and quality education. *Journal of Human Development, 7*, 385–395. https://doi.org/10.1080/14649880600815974.

Nwanji, N. (2023, September 22). *Over 76% of chief diversity officers are White while just under 4% are Black, report says*. YahooFinance. Accessed on March 1, 2024, from https://finance.yahoo.com/news/over-76-chief-diversity-officer-185454530.html.

O'Dowd, R. (2020). A transnational model of virtual exchange for global citizenship education. *Language Teaching, 53*(4), 477–490.

OECD. (2018). *Preparing our youth for an inclusive and sustainable world: The OECD PISA global competence framework*. Paris: OECD. Accessed on May 1, 2022, from www.oecd.org/education/Global-competency-for-an-inclusive-world.pdf.

Onyeador, I. N., Hudson, S. T. J., & Lewis, N. A. (2021). Moving beyond implicit bias training: Policy insights for increasing organizational diversity. *Policy Insights from the Behavioral and Brain Sciences, 8*(1), 19–26. https://doi.org/10.1177/2372732220983840.

Ortloff, D. H. (2011). Moving the borders: Multiculturalism and global citizenship in the German social studies classroom. *Educational Research, 53*(2), 137–149.

Palpacuer-Lee, C., Hutchison Curtis, J., & Curran, M. E. (2018). Stories of engagement: Pre-service language teachers negotiate intercultural citizenship in a community-based English language program. *Language Teaching Research, 22*(5), 590–607. https://doi.org/10.1177/1362168817718578.

Passarelli, A., & Kolb, D. A. (2012). Using experiential learning theory to promote student learning and development in programs of education abroad. In M. Vande Berg, R. M. Paige, & K. H. Lou (Eds.), *Student Learning Abroad: What Our Students Are Learning, What They're Not, and What We Can Do about It* (pp. 137–161). Sterling, VA: Stylus.

Peck, J. (2015). (Neo) liberalism, popular media, and the political struggle for the future of US-public education. *European Journal of Communication, 30*, 587–603. https://doi.org/10.1177/0267323115597853.

Pennamon, T. (2018). *Health insurance remains an issue for students and recent grads*. Diverse Issues in Higher Education. Accessed on December 10, 2023, from https://diverseeducation.com/article/117547/#:~:text=A%20nationwide%20poll%20by%20AgileHealthInsurancecosts%20as%20impediments%20to%20affordability.

Peraza, A. V. F., & Furumura, Y. (2022). Project-based learning to develop intercultural communicative competence in virtual exchange contexts.

International Journal of Computer-Assisted Language Learning and Teaching (IJCALLT), 12(3), 1–17.

Porto, M. (2019). Does education for intercultural citizenship lead to language learning? *Language, Culture and Curriculum, 32*(1), 16–33.

Porto, M., Golubeva, I., & Byram, M. (2023). Channelling discomfort through the arts: A Covid-19 case study through an intercultural telecollaboration project. *Language Teaching Research, 27*(2), 276–298. https://doi.org/10.1177/13621688211058245.

Porto, M., Houghton, S. A., & Byram, M. (2018). Intercultural citizenship in the (foreign) language classroom. Editorial. *Language Teaching Research, 22*(5), 484–498.

Porto, M., & Yulita, L. (2017). Language and intercultural citizenship education for a culture of peace: The Malvinas/Falklands Project. In M. Byram, I. Golubeva, H. Han, & M. Wagner (Eds.), *From Principles to Practice in Education for Intercultural Citizenship* (pp. 199–224). Bristol: Multilingual Matters.

Quaye, S. J., & Harper, S. R. (Eds.) (2015). *Student Engagement in Higher Education. 2nd Edition.* New York: Routledge.

Quorum. (2023). *Women in the 116th Congress.* Quorum. Accessed on December 1, 2023, from www.quorum.us/data-driven-insights/women-in-116th-congress/401/.

Ra, J. J., Boonsuk, Y., & Sangiamchit, C. (2022). Intercultural citizenship development: A case of Thai study abroad students in EMI programs. *Journal of English as a Lingua Franca, 11*(1), 89–104.

Rae, A. (2023, August 17). *DEI fatigue: Resistance or opportunity? Unpacking this moment And navigating the path forward.* Forbes. Accessed on March 15, 2024, from www.forbes.com/sites/aparnarae/2023/08/17/dei-fatigue-resistance-or-opportunity-unpacking-this-moment-and-navigating-the-path-forward/?sh=7f5e6af455af.

Rauschert, P., & Byram, M. (2018). Service learning and intercultural citizenship in foreign-language education. *Cambridge Journal of Education, 48*(3), 353–369. https://doi.org/10.1080/0305764X.2017.1337722.

Rauschert, P., & Mustroph, C. (2022). Intercultural education through civic engagement: Service learning in the foreign language classroom. In T. McConachy, I. Golubeva, & M. Wagner (Eds.) *Intercultural Learning in Language Education and Beyond: Evolving Concepts, Perspectives and Practices* (pp. 149–167). Bristol: Multilingual Matters.

Risager, K. (2006). *Language and Culture: Global Flows and Local Complexity.* Clevedon: Multilingual Matters.

Risager, K. (2007). *Language and Culture Pedagogy: From a National to a Transnational Paradigm*. Clevedon: Multilingual Matters.

Rufo, C. F. (2023, February 9). DEI Cult; The University of South Florida turns left-wing racialism into a psychological conditioning program. *City Journal*. Accessed on August 20, 2024, from link.gale.com/apps/doc/A779940381/AONE?u=anon~43e2ef01&sid=googleScholar&xid=17a47d51.

Sandoval-Hernández, A., Isac, M. M., & Miranda, D. (2019). Measurement Strategy for SDG Global Indicator 4.7.1 and Thematic Indicators 4.7.4 and 4.7.5 using International LargeScale Assessments in Education. Proposal. UNESCO Institute for Statistics. http://gaml.uis.unesco.org/wpcontent/uploads/sites/2/2019/08/GAML6-REF-9-measurement-strategy-for-4.7.1-4.7.4-4.7.5.pdf.

Schraedley, M. K., Jenkins, J. J., Irelan, M., & Umana, M. (2021). The neoliberalization of higher education: Paradoxing students' basic needs at a Hispanic-Serving Institution. *Frontiers in Sustainable Food Systems*, 5. https://doi.org/10.3389/fsufs.2021.689499.

Schuessler, J., Hartocollis, A., Levenson, M., & Blinder, A. (2024, January 2). *Harvard President Resigns after Mounting Plagiarism Accusations*. The New York Times. Accessed on February 10, 2024, from www.nytimes.com/2024/01/02/us/harvard-claudine-gay-resigns.html?action=click&pgtype=Article&module=&state=default&region=footer&context=breakout_link_back_to_briefing.

Shore, L. M., Chung-Herrera, B. G., Dean, M. A., et al. (2009). Diversity in organizations: Where are we now and where are we going? *Human Resource Management Review*, *19*(2), 117–133.

Soylu Yalcinkaya, N., Estrada-Villalta, S., & Adams, G. (2017). The (biological or cultural) essence of essentialism: Implications for policy support among dominant and subordinated groups. *Frontiers in Psychology*, *8*, 900. https://doi.org/10.3389/fpsyg.2017.00900.

Spreng, R. N., McKinnon, M. C., Mar, R. A., & Levine, B. (2009). The Toronto empathy questionnaire: Scale development and initial validation of a factor-analytic solution to multiple empathy measures. *Journal of Personality Assessment*, *91*(1), 62–71. https://doi.org/10.1080/00223890802484381.

Stephan, W. G., Stephan, C. W., & Gudykunst, W. B. (1999). Anxiety in intergroup relations: A comparison of anxiety/uncertainty management theory and integrated threat theory. *International Journal of Intercultural Relations*, *23*(4), 613–628. https://doi.org/10.1016/s0147-1767(99)00012-7.

Streitwieser, B., & Light, G. (2016). The grand promise of global citizenship through study abroad: The student view. In E. Jones, R. Coelen, J. Beelen, &

H. Hans de Wit (Eds.), *Global and Local Internationalization* (pp. 67–73). Rotterdam: Brill.

Supreme Court of the United States (SCOTUS). (2023). Syllabus: Students for Fair Admissions, Inc. v. President and Fellows of Harvard College. Accessed on March 15, 2024, from www.supremecourt.gov/opinions/22pdf/20-1199_hgdj.pdf.

Suter, A. (2024, April 25). DeSantis: Florida "will not comply" with new Biden Title IX rules. The Hill. Accessed on June 2, 2024, from https://thehill.com/homenews/lgbtq/4621642-desantis-florida-will-not-comply-with-new-biden-title-ix-rules/.

Tajfel, H., & Turner, J. C. (1979). An integrative theory of intergroup conflict. In W. G. Austin, & S. Worchel (Eds.), *The Social Psychology of Intergroup Relations* (pp. 33–47). Monterey, CA: Brooks/Cole.

Tenenbaum, H. R., Ingoglia, S., Wiium, N., et al. (2023). Can we increase children's rights endorsement and knowledge?: A pilot study based on the reference framework of competences for democratic culture. *European Journal of Developmental Psychology, 20*(6), 1042–1059. https://doi.org/10.1080/17405629.2022.2095367.

Ting-Toomey, S., & Kurogi, A. (1998). Facework competence in intercultural conflict: An updated face-negotiation theory. *International Journal of Intercultural Relations, 22*(2), 187–225. https://doi.org/10.1016/s0147-1767(98)00004-2.

Title VII of the Civil Rights Act of 1964 (Pub. L. 88–352) (2020).

Title IX of the Education Amendments Act of 1972, 20 U.S.C. §§1681–1688 (2018).

Tomlinson, B. (2018). *Undermining Intersectionality: The Perils of Powerblind Feminism*. Philadelphia, PA: Temple University Press.

Trapè, R. (2019). Building empathy and intercultural citizenship through a virtual exchange project. *Le Simplegadi XVII*(19), 167–180.

UNDP. (2018). *Sustainable development goals*. United Nations Development Programme. Accessed on March 30, 2024, from www.undp.org/content/undp/en/home/sustainable-development-goals.html.

UNESCO. (2012). *Education for sustainable development: Building a better, fairer world for the 21st century*. Accessed on May 3, 2023, from https://unesdoc.unesco.org/ark:/48223/pf0000216673.

UNESCO. (2014). *Global Citizenship Education: Preparing Learners for the Challenges of the 21st Century*. Paris: UNESCO.

University of Iowa (UI). (2022). Campus climate survey. Full Report. Accessed on February 22, 2024, from https://diversity.uiowa.edu/data/campus-climate-2022.

University of Michigan Library. (n.d.). *Online exhibits: Activism*. Accessed on March 30, 2024, from https://apps.lib.umich.edu/online-exhibits/exhibits/show/history-of-race-at-um/diversity-in-student-life/activism.

U.S. Bureau of Labor Statistics. (2023). *Employment status of the civilian noninstitutional population 25 years and over by educational attainment, sex, race, and Hispanic or Latino ethnicity*. Accessed on March 15, 2024, from www.bls.gov/cps/cpsaat07.htm.

Vaughn, B. E. (2007). The history of diversity training & its pioneers. *Strategic Diversity & Inclusion Management Magazine*, *1*(1), 11–16.

Veraksa, N., Basseches, M., & Brandão, A. (2022). Dialectical thinking: A proposed foundation for a post-modern psychology. *Frontiers in Psychology*, *13*, 710815. https://doi.org/10.3389/fpsyg.2022.710815.

Wagner, M., Cardetti, F., & Byram, M. (2019). *Teaching Intercultural Citizenship across the Curriculum: The Role of Language Education*. Alexandria, VA: American Council on the Teaching of Foreign Languages.

Warner, J., Ellmann, N., & Boesch, D. (2018, November 20). *The women's leadership gap*. Center for American Progress. Accessed on November 10, 2023 from www.americanprogress.org/article/womens-leadership-gap-2/.

Warren, C. J. E. (1954). Brown v. Board of Education. *United States Reports*, *347*, 483.

Willingham, S. (2022). *The root cause of diversity, equity and inclusion burnout, and how to fight it*. Forbes. Accessed on March 15, 2024, from www.forbes.com/sites/forbescoachescouncil/2022/08/16/the-root-cause-of-diversity-equity-and-inclusion-burnout-and-how-to-fight-it/?sh=6347dbed268c.

Woodin, J., Lundgren, U., and Castro, P. (2011). Tracking the traces of intercultural dialogue in internationalization policies of three EU universities: Towards a framework. *European Journal of Higher Education*, *1*(2–3), 119–134. https://doi.org/10.1080/21568235.2011.629038.

Zarya, V. (2018, May 21). *The share of female CEOs in the fortune 500 dropped by 25% in 2018*. Fortune. Accessed on March 15, 2024, from http://fortune.com/2018/05/21/women-fortune-500-2018/.

Zheng, L. (2022). *DEI Deconstructed: Your No-Nonsense Guide to Doing the Work and Doing It Right*. Oakland, CA: Berrett-Koehler.

Acknowledgments

First and foremost, I extend my sincere gratitude to my mentors, Martyn Barrett and Mike Byram, for their invaluable insights. I want to acknowledge my past and present co-authors, who have been wonderful collaborators in exploring the pedagogics of intercultural citizenship education and social justice. This research is collaborative in nature, and I am deeply thankful for having enthusiastic colleagues at my home institution and beyond. In particular, I would like to acknowledge (in alphabetic order) my colleagues, students, and research assistants who contributed in varied ways to research projects highlighted in this Element: Elizabeth Arevalo-Guerrero, Danielle Barefoot, Samantha Benton, David Di Maria, Shivam P. Gohel, Adam Holden, Petra Janka, Katherine Kohler, Jasmine Lee, Caylie Middleton, Kimberly Miller, Collin Sullivan, and Mary Ellen Wade.

I want to express special thanks to the editors of this volume – Will Baker, Troy McConachy, and Sonia Morán Panero – for their guidance, and to the peer reviewers for insightful feedback. My sincere appreciation also goes to my students and research assistants for their willingness to participate in my research projects.

I am also deeply grateful to Norbert, Daniel, and Petra for their understanding, patience, and support.

To my amazing parents, Ludmila and Valentin:
Thank you for your unwavering support and for being my true moral exemplars

Cambridge Elements

Intercultural Communication

Will Baker
University of Southampton

Will Baker is Director of the Centre for Global Englishes and an Associate Professor of Applied Linguistics, University of Southampton. His research interests are Intercultural and Transcultural Communication, English as a Lingua Franca, English medium education, Intercultural education and ELT, and he has published and presented internationally in all these areas. Recent publications include: *Intercultural and Transcultural Awareness in Language Teaching* (2022), co-author of *Transcultural Communication through Global Englishes* (2021), co-editor of *The Routledge Handbook of English as a Lingua Franca* (2018). He is also co-editor of the book series 'Developments in English as Lingua Franca'.

Troy McConachy
University of New South Wales, Australia

Troy McConachy is Senior Lecturer in the School of Education at University of New South Wales. His work aims to make interdisciplinary connections between the fields of (language) education and intercultural communication, focusing particularly on the role of metapragmatic awareness in intercultural communication and intercultural learning. He has published articles in journals such as ELT Journal, Language Awareness, Intercultural Education, the Language Learning Journal, Journal of International and Intercultural Communication, Journal of Intercultural Communication Research, and others. His is author of the monograph *Developing Intercultural Perspectives on Language Use: Exploring Pragmatics and Culture in Foreign Language Learning* (Multilingual Matters), and he has co-edited *Teaching and Learning Second Language Pragmatics for Intercultural Understanding* (with Tony Liddicoat), and *Negotiating Intercultural Relations: Insights from Linguistics, Psychology, and Intercultural Education* (with Perry Hinton). He is also Founding Editor and former Editor-in-Chief (2017–2024) of the international journal Intercultural Communication Education (Castledown).

Sonia Morán Panero
University of Southampton

Sonia Morán Panero is a Lecturer in Applied Linguistics at the University of Southampton. Her academic expertise is on the sociolinguistics of the use and learning of English for transcultural communication purposes. Her work has focused particularly on language ideologies around Spanish and English as global languages, English language policies and education in Spanish speaking settings and English medium instruction on global education. She has published on these areas through international knowledge dissemination platforms such as ELTJ, JELF, *The Routledge Handbook of English as a Lingua Franca* (2018) and the British Council.

Editorial Board
Zhu Hua, *University of Birmingham*
Ali Abdi, *The University of British Columbia*
Tomokazu Ishikawa, *Tamagawa University*
Ron Darvin, *The University of British Columbia*
Anne Kankaanranta, *Aalto University*
Xiaodong Dai, *Shanghai Normal University*
Sender Dovchin, *Curtin University*
Phan Le Ha, *University of Hawaii and Universiti Brunei Darussalam*
Jose Aldemar Alvarez Valencia, *Universidad del Valle*

About the Series
This series offers a mixture of key texts and innovative research publications from established and emerging scholars which represent the depth and diversity of current intercultural communication research and suggest new directions for the field.

Cambridge Elements

Intercultural Communication

Elements in the Series

Translingual Discrimination
Sender Dovchin

Short-Term Student Exchanges and Intercultural Learning
Gareth Humphreys

Intercultural Communication and Identity
Ron Darvin and Tongle Sun

Ethical Global Citizenship Education
Emiliano Bosio

Intercultural Communication in Virtual Exchange
Francesca Helm

Diversity, Equity, Inclusion and Intercultural Citizenship in Higher Education
Irina Golubeva

A full series listing is available at: www.cambridge.org/EIIC

www.ingramcontent.com/pod-product-compliance
Ingram Content Group UK Ltd.
Pitfield, Milton Keynes, MK11 3LW, UK
UKHW052320160225
455193UK00024BA/406